CW00505707

Beatnik

PO Box 8276, Symonds Street,
Auckland 1150, New Zealand

www.beatnikpublishing.com

First published in 2022 by Beatnik Publishing

Recipes: © 2022 Angelo Georgalli

Text: © 2022 Angelo Georgalli & Carla Munro
Text: © 2022 Fish & Game New Zealand

Photography: © Richard Cosgrove for Fish & Game New Zealand
Food Photography: © Sally Greer

Design, Typesetting, Cover & Illustrations: © 2022 Beatnik Publishing
Creative Director: Sally Greer
Designer: Kitki Tong

Recipe Development Assistant: Sky Horton

ISBN 978-0-9951423-7-4

FSC
www.fsc.org
MIX
Paper from
responsible sources
FSC™ C007683

Printed and bound in China on Forest Stewardship Council® (FSC®)–certified paper and other controlled material in a BSCI and SEDEX certified workplace.

Fish & Game
NEW ZEALAND

www.fishandgame.org.nz

THE
FISH+GAME
COOKBOOK

ANGELO GEORGALLI

CONTENTS

MALLARD/GREY
p.43

PARADISE SHELDUCK
p.61

SHOVELER
p.77

PŪKEKO
p.85

BLACK SWAN
p.95

FOREWORD
BY DAME LYNDA TOPP

It was a beautiful summer's morning in Methven, South Island, when Angelo pulled up to Topp Country Cafe. He came in, introduced himself as "the Game Chef", and ordered three poached eggs on a bed of spinach. I was cooking that day and I nervously dropped three free-range eggs into the swirling water.

Afterwards, as we chatted about hunting and cooking, he told me mine were the best poached eggs he'd ever had. It made me smile. That's the kind of chef Angelo is: giving, humble and awe-inspiring.

With the support of Fish & Game New Zealand – which manages, maintains and enhances sport fishing and game birds and their habitat – Angelo has taken game bird and fish recipes to the next level in this new book.

Now don't get me wrong, there's nothing like a roast duck with an orange stuffed up its bum, but Angelo brings us new ways of preparing and adding unbelievable flavours to our wild meats and fish.

It is also very exciting for me, as a trustee of the newly formed group Hunters For Conservation, to see Fish & Game pairing with the Game Chef. All of us can do our bit to work in with each other to manage and maintain the incredible gift of hunting and fishing that Aotearoa offers.

I have two beautiful hunting labs – Dream and Rosie – and it is a joy to watch them work on a frosty winter's morning on opening weekend of duck shooting; and the thrill of casting to a big brown in a clear South Island river never fails to excite me.

So get out there into the wilds and enjoy this amazing place we have, where we can provide our families with food on the table. And use this exciting cookbook to join Angelo and Fish & Game in also getting wild in the kitchen.

Dame Lynda Topp
Entertainer, Hunter, Fisherwoman
Cook and Trustee - Hunters for Conservation

INTRODUCTION

A man in the wilderness, at one with nature. Listening and tuning into the world around him and really appreciating the amazing abundance of nature. That's who I've been since writing *Angelo's Wild Kitchen*. A man in the wilderness.

So much has happened in those few years, but one of the most important things for me has been my own personal journey with where I'm at in life, my mental wellbeing, and my relationship with the beautiful wilderness we have right here on our doorstep in New Zealand. Not long after writing *Angelo's Wild Kitchen*, I became an honorary ranger for Fish & Game. It was an experience I both relished and cherished.

The team at Fish & Game are custodians, guardians, guides, and sages. At least, that's how I came to see them! They are local men and women who love being outdoors, have a deep respect for our lakes, rivers, forests, and mountains, and love to share their passion with as many Kiwis as they can. It felt only natural that I joined their ranks.

While Fish & Game is a not-for-profit organisation, they sure as heck give their all in helping get people into the wild safely. Fishing and hunting licences are such a small part of what they do. They help manage and maintain the habitats of the fish and game birds we hunt, ensuring that the environment is looked after and will still be there for generations to come. I've met some amazing people in my time as a ranger and hope I've helped instil a love of fishing and hunting in the people

I've dealt with, whether they were beginners or old hands. There's always a good yarn to spin when you meet like-minded people!

One of the first things I realised was how many others naturally live and align with my wild kitchen philosophy without even noticing it! These men and women I met, trained with, and shared stories with (you know, 'the big one' stories!), they naturally think the way I do about nature, wildlife, fishing, hunting, foraging, and taking care of the environment for our kids and grandkids to enjoy. It was amazing for me to find myself surrounded by people who 'get it'. You know, who have such deep respect for this incredible land, the rivers and the lakes, and the animals we hunt and fish to honour and to eat.

Being around other people who believed in the things I believe in helped me see that where I was in life wasn't where I thought I wanted to be. Working with Fish & Game helped me understand that it was the simpler things, those moments when I hooked a glorious rainbow and cooked it over an open fire by the river – these are the moments I cherished. The moments that really filled me up with joy. And it made me see that I wasn't truly happy with the busy, crazy, full-on lifestyle I had made for myself.

I had to come to terms with my own mental wellbeing and to allow myself to recognise that I couldn't do everything or be everything for other people. That I had to take care of myself. And for me, that was being in nature. with a rod in my hand on a river, or in the wild, just me and my quarry.

My journey with Fish & Game helped me on my journey back to being healthy, both physically and mentally. Fishing, hunting, playing with recipes and flavours. Working out, going for hikes, doing yoga, and getting out and enjoying this beautiful landscape we are so lucky to have in New Zealand. Just heading out the door to a park or a beach or a nature reserve as often as you can; it's so good for the soul. We have so much beauty and peace right on our doorstep, and I'd let myself forget it for too long.

Spending more time out there on a river or in the bush, truly being in that moment in time, and smiling because where you are right now is actually pretty good - it's what life is all about. Especially if you just hooked a beautiful big trout. Balance. Quiet times or fun times with friends or family. And getting out into the wild as often as you can!

I've given myself time to enjoy cooking and to experiment with recipes and with ways to really bring out the flavours and the value of wild game. To keep searching and foraging for seasonal ingredients that grow naturally in the environment. To keep pushing myself to discover new ways to enrich my recipes and introduce these amazing flavours and benefits to people. I guess that's what this cookbook is all about. First of all, it's a huge thank you to the Fish & Game team who make it possible for us to all enjoy the wilderness of this beautiful country. And secondly, it's a way to share my delicious experiments with the bounty we have in abundance on our doorstep. Some of these recipes take a bit of time, but it's time we should be taking to enjoy the process, to immerse ourselves in the joy of cooking and preparing a meal for those we love or just for ourselves. There's too much rushing around and fast fixes these days. Again, I bring it back to balance. The balance of the simple things in life and the things that take time and should take time. This cookbook is a real celebration of everything I stand for and everything the awesome team at Fish & Game stand for – harmony with nature and taking the time to enjoy the simple things, and to cook and share these recipes! I hope you enjoy cooking them as much as I have enjoyed creating them.

– Angelo

FISH & GAME
NEW ZEALAND

Rain often doesn't bring around good fortune for hunters and anglers but for readers of this cookbook, a bit of West Coast rain was the genesis of this project.

Angelo was reconnecting with nature when the West Coast "sunshine", known to non-coasters as heavy rain, started to fall.

Deciding to avoid the weather, he headed over the Southern Alps, and as he drove, he imagined a creative collaboration connecting the journey from lure to plate, maimai (hunting hide) to table.

Driving past the North Canterbury Fish & Game office, Angelo peeled off the motorway and popped in to sound out his idea with the team at Fish & Game.

Like all great ideas, this one gathered a head of steam and, almost a year later, has manifested itself in the book you hold in your hands.

But it wouldn't have happened without a great deal of help from the staff and wider Fish & Game 'family' around New Zealand.

Without their willingness to help and share their knowledge, this cookbook would have fallen flat like a bad soufflé.

But, like all hunters and anglers in New Zealand, they have inherited from their forebears a desire to feed their whānau with the best free-range food in the world.

They wanted to share their love for the wild game and freshwater fish in New Zealand and pitched in (often at short notice!) to make this book a success.

– Steve Doughty, Fish & Game New Zealand

FISH & GAME'S STORY

New Zealand's sports fish and game birds have a long and lauded history: some are indigenous to New Zealand and have been hunted as food for centuries first by Māori and later also by Pākehā colonists, whilst others were brought by Pākeha seeking to recreate aspects of Britain, realise social aspirations and provide a source of food.

All of New Zealand's freshwater sports fish are introduced, with the majority of introductions made as part of the acclimatisation movement in the mid-late 19th century. Beginning in Auckland in 1861, with the inception of the Auckland Acclimatisation Society, acclimatisation mania swept across the country to the extent that within a couple of decades the acclimatisation network covered almost every inch of the country. This mania was founded on the belief that New Zealand's environment was devoid of key species that colonists aspired to hunt, fish and eat, and that this required rectifying.

On this basis, in 1867 the Canterbury Acclimatisation Society secured a supply of brown trout ova from Tasmania, which were packed in moss-lined wooden boxes, covered in ice and placed into the cool store of the ship for the trans-Tasman voyage. On October 10, 1867, in specially made ponds in the acclimatisation grounds in the Canterbury Botanical Gardens, the first brown trout in New Zealand hatched. The following year both Canterbury and Otago received further supplies of ova from Tasmania, and they were able to begin the process of distributing these around the country. Fishing for trout began in New Zealand in December 1874, when the Otago Acclimatisation Society opened four rivers up to angling. Licences were available from the society for £1, or about $143 in today's money.

Rainbow trout followed from California in 1877 or 1883; confusion as to which species the Auckland Acclimatisation Society had received in 1877 makes it impossible to determine which. Both rainbow and brown trout took to New Zealand's rivers and lakes almost immediately, and likely would not have required the systematic distributions that the acclimatisation societies undertook to reach their current distributions. Today they are found from the cooler bush-lined creeks and reservoirs in the Far North to the most southern tip of Te Waipounamu, making them accessible to every single New Zealander. Such is the quality of New Zealand's wild trout fishery that, in more typical times, thousands of anglers travel from around the world each year to take up the unique opportunity to sight fish for large trout in clear water.

Along with rainbow and brown trout, which are the backbone of New Zealand's non-migratory freshwater sports fishery, a huge array of other species were brought over, from perch and tench to brook trout to American whitefish to lake trout. The extent to which these species took to their new antipodean home varied, with perch becoming well established, brook trout existing in isolated pockets around the country, lake trout now present in just one lake and American whitefish not surviving at all.

The biggest freshwater aspiration of the societies, the introduction of Atlantic Salmon – dubbed the king of fishes – was, however, never realised. Despite numerous attempts, and fleeting success in the Waiau River system, Atlantic Salmon never took in New Zealand in any substantive sense. Their Pacific cousin, the Chinook salmon – today the basis of New Zealand's salmon fishery – first arrived in 1875, although runs were not regular until the early 1900s when the government established a hatchery on the Hakataramea River in the central South Island. The management of the salmon fishery was shared between acclimatisation societies and government departments, primarily the Marine Department, because of an aspiration to develop a commercial industry around the wild resource. After two brief stints of commercial fishing in the 1920s and 1940s, Chinook salmon were formally designated a recreational species and their management transferred exclusively to the acclimatisation societies in the early 1950s.

Chinook salmon are today farmed at numerous sites around the country, with the farms in the Mackenzie Country canals providing incredible recreational opportunity for anglers fishing for escapee salmon or the often-enormous trout that are beneficiaries of the supplemented feed.

Along with Chinook salmon, the rivers and lakes of the central South Island host a population of sockeye salmon introduced originally from Canada. These fish, while running to sea in their native range, have only survived as landlocked populations in New Zealand. Most commonly encountered by anglers late season as they move into rivers to spawn, complete with dramatic humped backs and bright red flanks, if they are caught earlier in the year while fresh and silver they are among the most prized eating salmon.

In contrast, the game birds that Fish & Game manages today comprise a mixture of indigenous species and species introduced by colonists as part of the acclimatisation movement. Pūtakitaki/paradise shelduck, pārera/grey duck, kuruwhengi/shoveler duck and pūkeko are all indigenous to New Zealand and provided an important source of food for Māori. Early colonists also hunted these birds for food and recreation, and native game seasons occurred alongside introduced game seasons administered by the acclimatisation societies until 1937, when the management of all game was transferred to the acclimatisation societies. For some indigenous game birds, habitat loss and other environmental factors have led to strong declines in population whilst for others, such as the paradise shelduck, land conversion and an abundance of crops have resulted in increasing populations and a wider distribution around the country.

Kakīānau/black swan exist in somewhat of a middle ground between indigenous and introduced; the indigenous New Zealand black swan went extinct prior to Pākeha settlement but in the 1860s they were reintroduced from Australia. Today a number of iwi hold special permits to exercise a customary harvest of black swan, in particular the eggs and young birds called 'flappers'.

Mallard ducks, perhaps the most sought-after table bird available to the New Zealand hunter, were first brought to New Zealand from Britain in 1867 but their substantive establishment was not until the introduction of American mallards in the 1930s. Again, it was the work of acclimatisation societies that drove these introductions, and the subsequent management of these birds. Upon arrival in New Zealand, mallards interbred significantly with the native grey duck, resulting in substantial numbers of hybridised 'greylards'. Population dynamics around the country have shifted substantially over the 20th and into the 21st centuries but mallard ducks remain the backbone of New Zealand's game bird hunting.

Amongst the earliest introductions of game birds to New Zealand were upland species such as pheasants, which arrived as early as 1842. As the acclimatisation societies became established in the 1860s, they took over the importation and management of these birds. Early successes gave way to quickly reducing populations and costly stocking programs. These days most birds released are done by private syndicates or commercial operations, however good public pheasant hunting opportunities for wild birds exist around the country. In a similar vein to black swan, a native quail existed in New Zealand at the time of Pākeha colonisation and was avidly hunted, however, numbers declined rapidly until it eventually went extinct in the 1870s. Californian quail, the predominant species in New Zealand, arrived in the 1860s and quickly established in a number of areas around the country.

In 1990 the acclimatisation societies that had for 130 years managed New Zealand's sports fish and game resource on behalf of the public were reborn as Fish & Game through an amendment to the Conservation Act; 24 acclimatisation societies became twelve regional Fish and Game Councils and one national council. These days the work of Fish & Game is focused more heavily on habitat protection and restoration, to the benefit of indigenous and valued introduced species alike. Introductions, primarily of trout, continue to

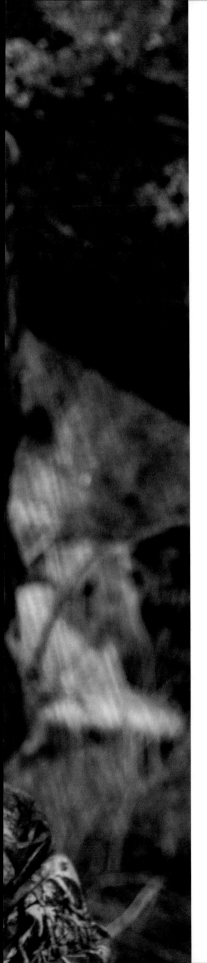

occur in areas where natural spawning is limited but for the most part sports fish and game birds in New Zealand are wild and self-sustaining; where there are healthy habitats there will be healthy populations. To achieve this, each year Fish and Game Councils submit on resource consent applications and regional plan change hearings, take legal action, submit on proposed legislation or regulations, and advocate generally to protect the habitat of sports fish and game. Through a combination of grass roots and national scale action, Fish & Game has proven to be one of the most effective environmental organisations in New Zealand, ensuring that future generations get to enjoy the same incredible hunting and fishing that we have now.

The species listed in this book are prized by countless New Zealanders, with Fish & Game licensing approximately 140,000 anglers and hunters every year. The extent of the connection to these pursuits varies, with many anglers and hunters having been raised with rod or shotgun in hand following in the footsteps of parents and grandparents alike. Others find hunting and fishing independently or through friends later in life, and yet value these species and what they represent no less than those who have grown up with them.

To Kiwis sports fishing and game bird hunting represent recreation, hobby and lifestyle. They provide an all-too-often overlooked connection to nature in truly stunning corners of New Zealand, and, most pertinent to the current situation, some of the finest free-range food to be found anywhere on the planet. There is truly no greater feeling on earth than sharing the rewards of hard work in the hills or on the water with family and friends around the dinner table at the end of the day.

– Dr Jack Kós, Fish & Game New Zealand

ANGELO'S TIPS & TRICKS

TIPS & TRICKS FOR COOKING WITH WATERFOWL & FISH

- Keep your catch cool! Whether it's fish or waterfowl, no one wants to eat green meat, not even the dog! Try to find cool, shady spots to hang birds until you get home or, if you can, take a cooler bag or chilly bin to keep caught or shot game fresh. Also, if you have time, best to gut your game first and hang if you can to drain.

- Keep your 'meat safe'. If you have a maimai or space at home, use a meat safe if possible to hang your catch/birds. They are great at allowing air to circulate and prevent flies or predators from contaminating your meat. If you want to keep them a bit longer, or if it's warmer than usual, hang your birds in a chilled environment below 4°C for a MAXIMUM of 10 days. This will help age the bird and tenderise the meat. Anything above this temp can spoil your meat and promote the growth of bacteria – the not-good kind!

- If you've had a good day out on the maimai or at the river, you might have a few extra birds or fish you want to freeze. Invest in a vacuum sealer. You can get some decent ones at your local appliance or homewares stores and it will make sure your precious meat maintains all those rich fresh flavours when frozen. Nothing worse than freezer burn!

- Give it a pat. Once plucked and cleaned, always pat your bird dry with a paper towel. You'll get a better result from your cooking.

- Marinating is all about submersion. Make sure the meat or fish is completely covered. This ensures all those amazing flavours and aromas are infused into the flesh and will ensure your finished dish tastes absolutely mind-blowing.

- When a recipe calls for meat or fish to be minced with some herbs but you don't have a mincer, you can use a blender or your trusty blitzer instead. If you don't have a blender, go old-school and finely chop the meat and herbs with a sharp knife.

- Always crush garlic before chopping. This breaks down the fibres in the clove and means easier chopping. Plus, the garlic flavours infuse more effectively into oil and/or meat.

- Allow meat/fish to rest for a few minutes after you take it off the barbecue grill or pan. This lets the juices settle and brings out the full flavour and tenderness of the meat.

- Because of the lack of fat in waterfowl, very slow or very fast cooking is the way to ensure a tender dish. For melt-in-your-mouth goodness make sure you follow the recipe guide for heat and cooking time, otherwise you could end up with a tough or chewy bird!

- Always check with Fish & Game or with local farmers to ensure no poisons have been released in or near the area you're fishing or shooting in.

- For cooking outdoors, make yourself a chefs pouch. Much like a builders apron, it keeps the tools of your trade like herbs, spices, oils, knives, and cutlery. Make sure you're prepared with plenty of water and make use of tinned ingredients and pre-packaged products to save valuable time.

- Broadly speaking, citrus – lemons, limes, oranges – and even kiwifruit are great with fish! The acidity of these fruits cooks the fish the moment the juice makes contact with the meat. That said, you'll often still want to cook the fish with some form of heat, but you'll get an awesome flavour boost from incorporating any citrus into your fish dishes!

- Always garnish to taste. If a recipe tells you to garnish with coriander, and you're not a fan, use something else or leave it out! For the coriander haters, use tarragon, parsley, basil or dill instead. Or go naked!

- To check if your roasting bird is done, use a thin sharp knife or a skewer and pierce the breast all the way to the breastplate. If it then bleeds red, give it a bit longer. If it's clear, it's done. Light pink juices are fine, but if there's no juice, whip it out of the oven quick or you'll end up with a dry bird!

- With game birds, to get the most out of the flavour and to add a bit of fat to them for cooking, make a herb butter of your favourite herbs and spices, and rub into or under the skin before cooking.

- Use fresh herbs wherever possible, but if they're not available substitute half a teaspoon of dried herbs to every handful of fresh herbs.

- If you want more kick (read: a lot more kick) in the recipes with chillies in them, you can opt not to deseed them. The seeds in chillies carry a lot of the heat, so if you're not going to deseed them, be warned!

- Save the planet and the flavour! I recommend using GLAD oven bags for my oven bag roasting dishes as they don't contain plasticisers, PVC or BPA, and they have recyclable packaging. Make sure you pierce a wee hole in the bag next to the tie to allow any build up of steam to find an exit point.

- When hot smoking, I like to add fresh rosemary and thyme to the woodchips to create a herbed aroma flavour.

- Baste it baby! To create a tender and flavoursome bird, baste at least three times during the cooking process.

- When checking if your fish is cooked, the flesh should appear opaque and, when pulled apart, flakes of flesh should fall away easily from the bone.

- When pin boning, I tend to use a clean pair of plyers or large tweezers. You'll find the pin bones down the centre of the salmon fillet. Pinch the exposed end of the bone with the tweezer and tug the bone away from the skin.

Can't go wild? Here are the best alternatives!

Waterfowl can be replaced with farmed duck which can be found in most supermarkets. Just be mindful that farmed duck requires less cooking time as they tend to have more natural fat.

Upland game can be replaced with free-range organic chicken.

Replicate the delicate flavours of quail with poussin. You may have to go to a specialist food market for this or your local butcher may know where to get it.

Freshwater trout and salmon can be replaced with farmed salmon. If you have a local fish market, give them a visit, or you can find salmon in the supermarket.

Fresh water perch can be replaced with blue cod, a southern favourite!

DISCLAIMER:

At the end of the day, the success of the dish comes down to you, the environment, and the quality of quarry.

A good hunter or angler knows that every bird or fish is different, as is the season, the environment, and the food that has nourished them.

As with all wild game, nabbing the right bird or fish is key to the success of the dish.

Waterfowl & Upland Game: If the bird is fatty and has been grazing on farmland then they're likely to be well suited to quick cooking such as pan frying. A wilder bird is likely to be lean and tougher so is more suited to low or slow cooking or roasting in an oven bag.

Freshwater Sports Fish: Generally speaking, fish are in their best condition after or at the beginning of the spawning season. This is because they've developed energy reserves in the run-up to spawning so have plenty of condition (fat) on them.

Large lakes and rivers with plenty of feed options and water flow tend to produce healthy, strong fish, and this is beautifully reflected in the flavour. As with birds, fish in good condition suit dishes that allow for the use of a whole fillet or they can be pan-seared. Leaner fish are better suited to pies, risottos or smoking.

To get the best out of my dishes, match the game to the cooking technique and you'll wow your dinner guests every time!

HOW TO PREPARE WATERFOWL & FISH FOR COOKING OR STORING

Kids and knives!: Always, always, always supervise kids when it comes to scaling, gutting, and filleting their catch. It's great to teach them how, but it's super important to also teach and guide them in the art of handling any sharp utensils, including a filleting knife! I'm of the opinion – and I'm going to stress here that this is my opinion, not a recommendation – that kids who learn to respect and understand how to use the tools needed to hunt and feed themselves are given a long-forgotten and valuable advantage in life. Being environmentally intelligent, knowing how to use and respect the land, water, sky, and all the creatures that we share this planet with is a gift your kids will thank you for. Oh and a little tip for you grown-ups as well – always keep your hands behind the blade!

WATERFOWL

Tip for all birds – gut them as soon as you can, even before plucking if possible. This means any spoiling of the meat is far less likely, for whatever reason! The innards, if punctured or damaged, can seep toxic juices into your carcass and ruin the meat.

DON'T BE GUTTED BY A BAD GUTTING JOB!

Gutting or eviscerating your game bird is not as hard as it sounds. But is does take a bit of delicacy. First of all, use a small, sharp knife (a filleting knife is good) and make a cut at the throat and below the breastplate. Insert a hose or tap into the throat cut and gently rinse the cavity. The breastplate cut needs to slice down towards the anus. Some hunters cut this part and the pope's nose (the end knob of the carcass) off at this point, but that's entirely up to you! Be extra careful not to slice into any of the entrails! This will spoil the meat and render it unusable.

Once you've got a nice, clean slit, reach in and gently remove the gizzard, heart, lungs and entrails. This feels a bit like being a surgeon and you get used to what you're feeling for the more often you do it! I then use a teaspoon handle or something similar as a scraper to remove any material attached on either side of the backbone. Now you're ready to give your bird a wee wash and voilà – you've got one good gutted bird!

PLUCK A DUCK! (OR ANY OTHER GAME BIRD...!)

Plucking a game bird might seem like an easy, if somewhat gruesome, task. But trust me, you can get this wrong!

Again, pluck as soon as you can and keep the bird dry if at all possible! The art of plucking a bird is to be firm but gentle at the same time. You don't want to rip the skin. Use your thumb and forefinger, take a firm grip of the feathers, and pull up and away from the skin. Pluck against the grain. This is more likely to get the feathers at the root and can be easier to get a cleaner pluck. Think about waxing – not that anyone here gets waxed! A wee side note on a few of our rarer feathered friends. Plucking upland game, such as pheasants, quail, peafowl, chickens or turkeys, can be made easier by first giving them a dunk in hot water. The consensus seems to be that water at around 60-70°C works best. Fifteen seconds or so should do it. Next, give the bird a rattle about in the bucket. The larger body feathers will come out more easily. Once you've the majority of the feathers off, you'll often be left with pinfeathers, the wee fluffy white under-feathers. The easiest way to get rid of these is to singe them off. You can use a propane blowtorch if you have one handy, or even a camping gas cooker will do the job. But if you're going super old-school, any kind of controlled flame should do the trick. Just be very careful with fire and have someone or something ready to put it out if it gets out of hand! Water, salt, an old towel – anything that will dampen fire.

Then you want to remove the outer, larger wings by cutting them off at the first joint. Use a sharp knife, gardening secateurs or a small axe to do this, and make sure you're careful. Lastly, remove the head and legs below the first joint in the same way. Give the bird a good rinse then dry it ready for gutting – if you haven't done this already.

BREASTING A DUCK (ALL VARIEITIES INCLUDING MALLARD, PARADISE, ETC)

To breast a duck, cut a slice across the base of the sternum of your freshly plucked bird, hold the feet and tail firmly, insert your fingers into the cut and grab hold of the base of the sternum, then pull up. You'll need to put a bit of energy into this! The aim is to take the sternum and the breast meat on either side all at once. When you've got the sternum and breast meat free, use a knife to cut it away from the ribs by cutting down the inside of the sternum towards the back bone. Then separate from the neck and head and tidy up and wash for cooking or freezing.

BREASTING A PŪKEKO (YEP, IT'S A LITTLE BIT DIFFERENT TO A DUCK!)

Ok, this is going to sound a bit full on, and trust me, breasting a pūkeko the easy way isn't for the faint-hearted or novice! It's quick, clean, and really works! Lay the bird, preferably still warm as this will make it easier, breast down on the ground, legs stretched out towards you. Pin the bird to the ground with your foot firmly on its legs then bend down and grab each wing base as close to the body as you can. Make sure your grip is tight and that your foot on the legs is firm, then simply – stand up. If you've held the wings firmly enough, you'll have a pair of wings and two skinned breasts in

your hands. Use a sharp knife to finish the job and remove the wings and tidy up any loose flesh, feather, or bone, store the meat and you're done. Make sure you dispose of the leftover carcass. If you have any trouble, make a couple of cuts just below the ribcage and repeat the process. As I said, easy! A big thanks to John Meikle from Fish & Game for this handy breasting tip!

BREAK IT DOWN - GETTING THE MOST OUT OF YOUR GAME BIRD

When it comes to any bird, I like to use as much of the meat as I possibly can. This method of breaking the bird down will work for ducks, swans, pheasants, turkeys – pretty much all larger game birds. Start with the legs. Press on the gap between the legs and breast and slice down that gap through the skin, cutting down until you reach the joint. As you slice, arc the knife under the thigh to get all the meat off the thigh. Snap the leg backwards to pop the socket and voilà – you have a leg! Wings are next. Look for the dark line where the breast ends, this is where to make your cut in a parallel slice all the way to the wing joint. Slide your knife along the saber bone, the long curved bone along the back, to the joint. Remove the wing by cutting a little extra skin from the neck area. Lastly, the breasts. If you take the breasts off in one piece, it wastes less skin, which in cooking, can protect the meat from drying out. Make a cut along the fatty pad on the side of the bird and slide your knife along the fat line to the tail, making sure you get all the meat along the breast plate. Once the back of the breast is free, run your knife along the bone at the neck end then along the wishbone up towards the keel bone. Think of it as freeing the meat rather than cutting or slicing it and work your knife carefully to get all the meat you can. Repeat on the other side, then gently cut away the attachments along the top of the keel. The tenders will still be attached at this point, and you can remove these if you want to sear or pan-fry the breast. You can still use these and the rest of the carcass to make amazing stocks and soups! There you go! Done!

FISH:

SCALING & GUTTING YOUR FISH

First of all, give your fish a good clean. I like to rinse it in fresh water – yes, I know it's just come out of water, but by giving it a hearty rinse you're washing away any remnants from the live fish. Then, regardless of the variety, take a firm hold of the tail in one hand and take your scaling or sharp knife (you can use your filleting knife for this) and scrape from tail to tip. The scales will peel away – yep, it can be a bit messy so set down some old newspaper if you're inside or scale outside. Repeat until you have a nice smooth skin then give it another decent rinse in fresh water.

To gut the fish, insert the point of your knife into the vent of the fish. The vent is a spot about 1-2 inches back from the base of the pectoral fin. The vent releases gases in the swim bladder. Be careful not to go too deep. You'll see a 'V' just below the mouth. Sweep the knife from the vent up to the top of the 'V' of the chin to where the blade meets hard cartilage.

FILLET A FISH (NOT TO BE CONFUSED WITH A FILET-O-FISH!)

If you're intending on filleting the fish you catch then you don't need to worry about scaling or even gutting it. Give it a good clean to get rid of any debris or any leftover trace of stress from the catch. Lay the fish on its side and make a cut behind its gills and another behind the pectoral fin down to the rib cage. You can remove the head, or leave it on. If you're going to use the rest of the fish for stock or paste, leave the head intact. Plenty of flavour to be had in the head. Turn the blade of your knife toward the tail and cut along the top of the ribs. You can use the backbone as a guide here. Once you've done that, turn the fish over and repeat! Then insert the knife close to the ribcage and slice away the whole rib section. Repeat on both sides. With the skin side facing down, make a cut about half an inch from the tail, grip the tail firmly, place the knife blade on a gentle angle between the skin and the flesh

and, using a bit of pressure and a slight sawing motion, slice away the skin. The fillet should come away nice and clean from the skin. Again, repeat on both sides. Give the fillets a nice wash in fresh water, pat dry, and you're ready to cook! Remember, if you're freezing fresh fillets, they need to be clean, dry, and preferably vacuum-sealed to keep the freshness and flavours intact.

BUTTERFLYING A FISH (NOT EVEN CLOSE TO HOW TO BUTTERFLY A LAMB LEG!)

Butterflying a fish is generally done for when you want to smoke it, but you can also cook a butterflied fish as well – best on the BBQ! Once you have scaled and gutted your fish, lay the fish on its back, not its sides, on a sturdy chopping board, take a firm hold of it, and with a sharp knife cut into the centre of the fish at the very top of the back bone. You'll need to be pretty firm with this, guys, and might even need to press or chop firmly to get the knife inserted. Once you've got a good hold in the top of the backbone inside the back of the head, continue cutting down the ridge of the back bone. It'll take a bit of elbow grease! Once you get down to the anal slice you made when gutting the fish, angle the knife to one side, the closest side to you, and run the knife alongside the backbone to the tail. Press it open with your hands and it should fold open like a butterfly! You can cut the head off if you like, that's totally up to you! What you end up with is a nice clean line straight down the centre of the fish and you should be able to see the skin through the cut. You can take the bone out at this point if you want to and feel free to tidy it up if it's going on the BBQ for friends! To remove the bone, run your knife along the edge of the base of the bone and carefully remove. I tend to leave the bones in however. It's so much easier to remove the bones once cooked. You'll find once you've cut along the edge of the trunk of the bone, you can just tug gently and the entire network of bones will lift away.

– Angelo, with help and guidance from John Dyer, John Meikle and Mark Sherburn, Fish & Game NZ

FAVES & FLAVOURS

1½ cups **soft brown sugar**
½ cup **red wine vinegar**
¼ cup **dried cranberries**
½ cup **water**
½ cup **diced prunes**
1½ Tbsp **Worcestershire sauce**
3 Tbsp **wholegrain mustard**
¼ tsp **cayenne pepper**
1 tsp **smoked paprika**
½ tsp **salt**
½ tsp **pepper**

CRANBERRY & PRUNE BBQ SAUCE

You can't beat a good BBQ sauce! So versatile, this tangy take on a saucy staple combines the sweet, plump, underrated goodness of the juicy prune and some of my favourite spices. And let's not forget cranberries! Not just for Christmas, I love the tart freshness of a cranberry – and they are chock full of vitamin C too.

In a saucepan on a medium heat, add the brown sugar, red wine vinegar, cranberries, water and prunes. Bring to the boil and simmer for 15 minutes, stirring occasionally.

Add Worcestershire sauce, wholegrain mustard, cayenne pepper, smoked paprika, salt and pepper, and stir briskly for a further 5 minutes. Once thickened, take it off the heat and let cool.

Serve or refrigerate in bottle jars for up to 2 weeks.

500g **blackberries**
5 Tbsp **caster sugar**
1 Tbsp **fig vincotto**
1 tsp **wholegrain mustard**
5 sprigs **thyme**
¼ tsp **coarse black pepper**
3 Tbsp **port**

BLACKBERRY & PORT SAUCE

Another winter favourite, blackberries add a tangy sweetness to any sauce. Rich and heady, the thyme gives this delectable sauce a rustic flair. Amazingly, the hills around Central Otago are abundant in wild thyme. The scent of it always reminds me of my Italian mother's cooking. Both thyme and blackberries have powerful antioxidant properties. Gotta love a good sweet sauce that's good for you.

In a hot saucepan add all ingredients together and simmer for 10 minutes or until thickened, stirring occasionally.

Serve with game birds or game meats for a rich complement to your meal.

TIP: this recipe tastes even better with freshly picked seasonal berries

10 minutes

 30 minutes

 Makes 375ml

1 cup **pitted cherries**
2 Tbsp **white sugar**
¼ tsp **orange zest**
Pinch of **nutmeg**
Pinch of **allspice**
Pinch of **cinnamon**
Pinch of **ground ginger**
Pinch of **dried rosemary**
½ clove **garlic**, minced
½ Tbsp **balsamic glaze**
3 Tbsp **fortified cherry wine**
3 Tbsp **brandy**
Pinch of **black pepper**

TO ADD AT THE END
4 Tbsp **fortified cherry wine**

CHERRY BRANDY SAUCE

Another magical sauce full of rich, decadent flavours. I'm lucky to live right on the cusp of Central Otago and every summer I make sure to get bags of fresh, fat, juicy cherries to use and freeze for cooking. They add a lush depth of flavour to this sauce. It tastes a little bit like Christmas!

In a pan on a low heat add all the ingredients and mix together until thickened (approx. 20 minutes), stirring occasionally.

Take off the heat and allow to cool. Blitz in a food processor adding a further 4 Tbsp of cherry wine.

Serve as a side garnish or drizzled over waterfowl.

 10 minutes

 20 minutes

 Makes 300ml

1 cup **blackberries**
10 **plums**, halved
3 Tbsp **caster sugar**
1 Tbsp **fig balsamic vinegar**
3 tsp **port**
2 tsp **Cointreau**
¼ tsp **vanilla paste**

BLACKBERRY & PLUM SAUCE

Wild blackberries still grow in many parts of New Zealand, particularly in the South Island. Sweeter than raspberries but with its own heady tang, the humble blackberry adds a richness to these delectable autumn flavours. Brilliantly flavourful and a perfect addition to any waterfowl dish.

Place all the ingredients into a saucepan on a medium/high heat for approx. 1-2 minutes and ensure all ingredients are mixed in.

Lower the heat and simmer for 15 minutes, stirring regularly.

Take off the heat and let it cool.

Put the mixture in a blender and blitz until smooth.

Enjoy heated through as a nice addition to any waterfowl dish.

5 minutes 20 minutes  Makes 400ml

1 Tbsp **butter**

1 Tbsp **light olive oil**

8 **sage leaves**

½ medium **white onion**, sliced

1 clove **garlic**, sliced

1 **bay leaf**

Salt & **pepper**

1 cup **frozen** or **fresh blueberries**

1 Tbsp **brown sugar**

1 tsp **wholegrain mustard**

¼ cup **red wine**

1 Tbsp **fig balsamic vinegar**

¼ cup **water**

BLUEBERRY & SAGE SAUCE

The aromatic essence of sage complements game birds nicely. Earthy and sweet, the combination of fresh sage and blueberries is a gently juicy taste phenomenon.

In a hot saucepan, heat the butter and olive oil. Once they're hot add the sage leaves and fry until crispy.

Add the onion, garlic, bay leaf, a pinch of salt and pepper, blueberries, brown sugar, wholegrain mustard, red wine and fig balsamic vinegar. Stir together, lastly adding ¼ cup of water. Reduce the heat to low-medium and simmer for 10 minutes or until thickened.

Serve with upland game and waterfowl.

TIP: *If using frozen blueberries, thaw them first before adding to the hot pan.*

 5 minutes 10-15 minutes Makes 1.3L

10 '**ready to eat**' **sundried figs**, diced

3 Tbsp **wholegrain mustard**

2 Tbsp **Worcestershire sauce**

1½ Tbsp **soft brown sugar**

1½ cups **tomato passata sauce**

½ cup **red wine vinegar**

½ cup **water**

1 tsp **smoked paprika**

1 tsp **salt**

1 tsp **coarse black pepper**

FIG BBQ SAUCE

The fig is an often underrated fruit, but I'm a little enamoured by it! It gives this smoky sweet sauce a tasty tartness, making it the perfect culinary companion for those blissful BBQ days!

In a hot pan, add all the ingredients and simmer for 10-15 minutes, stirring occasionally. Take off the heat, allow to cool.

Refrigerate in an airtight bottle or jar for up to 2 weeks.

The Fish & Game Cookbook | *Angelo Georgalli* | FAVES & FLAVOURS

5 minutes   25 minutes   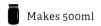 Makes 500ml

50g **butter**

1 **red onion**, diced

2 cloves **garlic**, chopped

1 **red capsicum**, diced

1 tsp **wholegrain mustard**

3 pinches of **salt**

3 pinches of **pepper**

3 **tamarillos**, peeled and chopped

1 Tbsp **balsamic glaze**

½ cup **orange juice**

2 Tbsp **apple syrup**

Salt & **pepper**

RICH RED TAMARILLO CHUTNEY

While tamarillos are in season from around March through to October in New Zealand, get into it and make up a few jars of this awesome chutney. So versatile, a good tasty chutney is brilliant for so many things. Add to casseroles or simply slather it on game meat for extra flavour. Spread on pancakes or warm crusty bread, there's just so much you can do with a good chutney!

In a hot saucepan add the butter and saute the onion, garlic and capsicum. Once softened, stir in the mustard, salt and pepper. Add the tamarillos, balsamic glaze and orange juice. Simmer until thickened for 15 -20 minutes, stirring occasionally.

Finally stir in the apple syrup and season with additional salt and pepper to taste.

Serve as a side with waterfowl.

 5 minutes   2 hours 35 minutes   Makes 1L

1 Tbsp **olive oil**

5 cloves **garlic**, crushed and chopped

2 x 410g tins **crushed tomatoes**

1 **chicken stock cube**

¼ cup **water**

3 pinches of **ground** or **coarse black pepper**

3 pinches of **salt**

¼ cup **extra virgin olive oil**

RUSTIC RAGU SAUCE

A ragu sauce is a rich, delicious, full-flavoured sauce that is traditionally used to cook meat. Think of it as a meaty tomato sauce. It goes well with pasta dishes, lasagne, casseroles, and stews.

In a large hot saucepan, brown the garlic in the olive oil. Add the tinned tomatoes to the saucepan, along with the chicken stock cube dissolved in the water. Season generously with salt and pepper and finish with a helping of olive oil.

Turn the heat down and simmer for 2 hours 30 minutes.

Serve hot.

10 minutes    10-15 minutes   Makes 1.2L

1½ cups **brown sugar**

1½ cups **passata tomato sauce**

½ cup **red wine vinegar**

½ cup **water**

½ cup **sundried apricots,** sliced

1½ Tbsp **Worcestershire sauce**

3 Tbsp **wholegrain mustard**

1 Tbsp **hot chilli pepper sauce**

1 tsp **smoked paprika**

½ tsp **salt**

½ tsp **pepper**

50ml **Bourbon**

APRICOT & BOURBON BBQ SAUCE

Game over flame! This special sauce has got a really cheeky Kentucky meets Central Otago flavour going on and is so good with barbequed meat of almost any kind!

In a saucepan, mix brown sugar, passata sauce, red wine vinegar, water and apricots. Bring to the boil, turn the heat down and simmer for 3-5 minutes, stirring regularly. Add Worcestershire sauce, wholegrain mustard, hot chilli pepper sauce, smoked paprika, salt and pepper. Next add the Bourbon. Stir briskly for another 5 minutes or so until thickened.

Serve over barbequed fillets and wings.

Will store in the fridge for up to a week.

 5 minutes   1 minute   Makes 260ml

1 tsp **mild curry powder**

¼ tsp **lemon pepper**

¼ tsp **ground coriander seeds**

¼ **red onion**, sliced

1 clove **garlic**, chopped

1 Tbsp **vegetable oil**

1 cup **Greek yoghurt**

1 tsp **runny honey**

1 tsp **lemon juice**

10 **mint leaves**, chopped

2 pinches of **salt**

SPICED MINT YOGHURT SAUCE

A perfect accompaniment to a wide range of dishes, this spicy, minty sauce is a little bit Greek, a little bit Indian, and a lot Angelo!

In a small bowl stir together the mild curry powder, lemon pepper and the ground coriander with the red onion and garlic.

Transfer into a small saucepan over a medium heat and brown in the pan with vegetable oil for a few seconds. Turn off the heat. Add the yoghurt, honey, lemon juice, mint leaves and salt. Stir to combine all the ingredients.

5 minutes   2-3 minutes   Makes 200ml

3 **egg yolks**

½ Tbsp **white vinegar**

Pinch of **lemon pepper**

150g **melted butter**

Zest of ½ **lemon**

6 drops **lemon juice**

1 Tbsp **fresh dill**, roughly chopped

LEMON & DILL HOLLANDAISE SAUCE

A fancy twist on a classic French sauce, the lemon zest and dill in this recipe keep the sauce light and give it a slight tang that complements the flavour of freshwater fish.

In a saucepan, bring to the boil 2 cups of water. Using a stainless steel or glass bowl, combine the egg yolks, vinegar and lemon pepper. Position the bowl so the base is sitting in the saucepan of hot water and whisk the egg yolks until they begin to thicken. Slowly add melted butter to the egg mixture, whisking as you go.

Add the lemon zest, juice and dill, and stir until the sauce is the consistency of runny custard. Remove the bowl from the saucepan and serve.

 5 minutes   3 minutes   Makes 450ml

1½ cups **Greek yoghurt**

1 clove **garlic**, finely chopped

½ of handful **mint**, finely chopped

½ **lemon**, juice and zest

¼ **cucumber**, chopped

Pinch of **smoked paprika**

Pinch of **turmeric**

Pinch of **cumin**

Salt & **pepper**

ANGELO'S FAMOUS TZATZIKI SAUCE

I wouldn't be half Greek if I didn't have my own version of a tzatziki sauce! And I'd be proud to serve this one to my Cypriot Greek family! The key to a great tzatziki – is fresh, organic, wholesome ingredients. Buy local and organic whenever you can.

Combine all the ingredients into a medium bowl and mix well. Add salt and pepper to taste.

5 minutes   45 minutes   Makes 1L

1 **fish carcass**

1L **boiling water**

3 Tbsp **salt**

Handful each of **rosemary, dill** and **parsley**

1 **onion**, halved

½ **lemon**

FISH STOCK

When filleting fish you're always left with such a large amount of waste. Making a fish stock is great way to use the whole fish. Plus you have the bonus of being able to use it in soups, curries, broth, puttanesca sauce and more. Full of goodness with essential vitamins and minerals, this resourceful recipe can freeze for up to 3 months. I recommend getting covered ice trays and freezing your fish stock in separate little cubes.

Fillet and gut your fish of choice, keeping the remaining carcass; head, tail, bones – the lot!

In a large stockpot, submerge the fish carcass in boiling water, and cover with a lid (1 fish carcass usually makes 1 litre of stock). Boil for 20 minutes. Scoop out any foam residues that float to the surface.

Add salt, herbs, onion and half a lemon. Boil for a further 25 minutes.

'Fish out' the carcass and sieve the stock into a bowl, removing any small bones and skin. Let cool.

Store in an airtight container and refrigerate for up to a week.

 5 minutes   15 minutes    Makes 300ml

1½ **chicken stock cubes**

200ml **hot water**

30g **unsalted butter**

½ **small white onion**, finely diced

1 clove **garlic**, finely diced

2 sprigs **rosemary**, destalked and finely chopped

1 pinch of **dried thyme**

1 Tbsp **Worcestershire sauce**

1 Tbsp **date syrup**

3 pinches of **Up Your Game Pepper Steak Seasoning** (see page 39)

2 tsp **maize cornflour**

¼ cup **cold water**

THE UPLAND GRAVY BABY

For the perfect gravy ALWAYS add the juices from the meat you are cooking. It's a game changer!

Dissolve the chicken stock cubes in hot water and set aside.

In a hot frying pan, melt the butter and add the onion and garlic and lightly brown for 2-3 minutes. Throw in the rosemary, thyme and Worcestershire sauce along with the date syrup. Turn the heat down to a simmer stirring regularly for 4-5 minutes. Add your chicken stock and pepper steak seasoning. Stir well.

Dissolve the maize cornflour in the cold water. Add the liquid to the pan and stir in to thicken the sauce. This will create your gravy consistency.

Serve warm.

5 minutes   5 minutes   Makes 625g

4 **Lebanese cucumbers**

1 cup **apple cider vinegar**

3 **spring onion stalks**

1 clove **garlic**, chopped

5 fronds **dill**

½ tsp **yellow mustard seeds**

1 tsp **kosher salt**

¼ tsp **fennel seeds**

1 **bay leaf**

5 whole **gourmet pepper corns**

2 tsp **soft brown sugar**

PICKLED CUCUMBER

Let's get pickled! I bet you didn't know how easy it is to pickle your own cucumber? Well, it is! And they can be used in so many ways, are delicious, and so good for you! Pickle up your salads, antipasto boards, sandwiches, burgers and more! Gives a punchy bite to any meal.

In a large bowl, shave the cucumbers using a potato peeler, then slice the white part of the spring onion length ways. Add the garlic and set aside.

In a hot saucepan add the vinegar, dill, mustard seeds, kosher salt, fennel seeds, bay leaf and peppercorns. Bring to the boil then turn the heat down, simmering for 1 minute. Take off the heat and stir in the brown sugar until dissolved. Set this brine water aside to cool.

Into a jar, add the cucumbers, spring onion and garlic. Pour in the brine water. There you have it, pickled cucumber in a jar.

Seal the jar tight and refrigerate for at least 12 hours before serving.

 5 minutes   Makes 200g

40g **fresh ginger**

3 cloves **garlic**

2 whole **tomatoes**

1 whole **red chilli**

3 Tbsp **vegetable oil**

1 tsp **hot curry powder**

Handful of **fresh coriander leaves**

3 pinches of **ground cumin**

3 pinches of **ground turmeric**

3 pinches of **fennel seeds**

3 pinches of **cayenne pepper**

2 pinches of **ground coriander seeds**

2 pinches of **Chinese five spice**

2 pinches of **black pepper**

1 pinch of **saffron**

FISH RUB

Another staple for the fridge. Fish Rub is used in a wide range of dishes to add flavour, depth, and zingy goodness. It also honours the fish by using as much of it as you can.

Add all the paste ingredients into a food processor and blend until a coarse consistency is achieved.

Empty into an airtight container and refrigerate for up to a week.

5 minutes   1 hour   Makes 400ml

1L **Foundation beef stock**
1 cup **good drinking red wine**
1 **carrot**, sliced
1 clove **garlic**, crushed
1 **bay leaf**
4 sprigs **fresh thyme**
4 sprigs **parsley**
2 sprigs **oregano**
1 sprig **fresh rosemary**
2 Tbsp **soft brown sugar**

RED WINE JUS

A good, homemade red wine jus just cannot be beaten for hearty, rich, decadent flavour. Drizzled over red meat or, in this cookbook, dark game birds such as black swan, the jus brings wild flavours to life, enhancing and emboldening dishes.

In a saucepan on a medium heat, add all the ingredients and simmer for 35 minutes. Test to see if it's ready by dipping a spoon into the pan; if it forms a sticky glaze over the spoon then it's ready. Strain the solution into a saucepan, removing the herbs, vegetables etc. leaving a smooth liquid.

Place the saucepan back on the heat for a further 20 minutes. Test it's ready by using the spoon method as before, this time it should be even thicker in consistency as it glazes the back of a spoon.

Serve with waterfowl or red meat.

TIP: It really is essential to use a good quality beef stock to achieve a beautiful jus. I swear by using Foundation Beef stock as my secret ingredient to making this jus unforgettable.

 5 minutes   5 minutes   Makes 530ml

1 x 400g **can chickpeas**
½ cup **fresh baby spinach**
2-3 Tbsp **water**
1 Tbsp **extra virgin olive oil**
1 clove **garlic**, minced
½ tsp **ground cumin**
¼ cup **lemon juice**
¼ cup **white tahini**
¼ tsp **salt**
Pinch of **smoked paprika**

SPINACH HUMMUS

Once you've made fresh homemade hummus, you won't go back to store bought stuff. Enough said.

Place all the ingredients into a blender.

Carefully secure the lid and blend on pulse for 30 seconds or until smooth.

Store in an airtight container and refrigerate for up to 7 days. But trust me, it won't last long in the fridge!

TIP: If you want to make your own tahini, combine ¼ cup white sesame seeds with 2 Tbsp olive oil and mix in a blender until a creamy paste is formed, approx. 5 minutes.

1 Tbsp **gourmet peppercorns**

¼ tsp **ground turmeric**

¼ tsp **ground coriander seeds**

¼ tsp **ground cinnamon**

¼ tsp **smoked paprika**

1 Tbsp **natural coarse sea salt**

1 clove **garlic**

½ tsp **fresh thyme**, chopped

½ tsp **fresh rosemary**, chopped

1 tsp **olive oil**

RUB-A-DUB DUCKIE RUB

Everyone likes a good rub-a-dub-dub! I created this one specifically to complement the wilder flavours of waterfowl. I only use the good spices – I promise!

Using a mortar & pestle, grind the peppercorns into a fine powder - this will help the rub stick to the bird. Add the turmeric, coriander, cinnamon and paprika. Mix together and set aside.

Using the mortar & pestle, grind the salt, garlic, thyme, rosemary and olive oil into a fine/medium paste.

Add the dried spice mix and combine well.

Rub onto any waterfowl meat.

2 tsp **panko breadcrumbs**

1 tsp **almonds**, crushed

1 tsp **mild curry powder**

½ tsp **dried dill**

½ tsp **marjoram**

¼ tsp **garlic powder**

¼ tsp **lemon pepper**

3 pinches of **salt**

3 pinches of **pepper**

CURRY IN A HURRY CRUMBED RUB

If friends or unexpected guests arrive, this is a must-have pantry staple to impress them at the last minute. Absolutely brilliant for giving any pan-fried fish a flavoursome punch.

Mix all the ingredients together in a small bowl and store in an airtight container.

Use this beautiful dish enhancer as a rub or seasoning with upland game birds.

Store in a cool dry container for up to 6 months.

5 minutes

 45 minutes

 Makes 25g

2 tsp **panko breadcrumbs**
1 tsp **pistachios**, crushed
1 tsp **black sesame seeds**
¼ tsp **ground coriander seeds**
¼ tsp **smoked paprika**
¼ tsp **ground cumin**
¼ tsp **ground ginger**
¼ tsp **dried mint**
3 pinches of **salt**
3 pinches of **pepper**

MIDDLE MEATS EAST CRUMBED RUB

The exotic aromas of this vivid crumbed rub will transport you to the Egyptian spice markets. With vibrant colour and equally vibrant flavour, this is a striking addition to your bird or fish dish.

In a bowl, mix all the ingredients together.

Store in an airtight container. Easy as that!

Use as a crumb or rub to complement fish and game birds for a Middle Eastern flavour.

 5 minutes

 Makes 20g

2 cloves **garlic**
1 tsp **Chinese five spice**
1 tsp **coriander seeds**
½ tsp **dried ginger**
½ tsp **sesame seed oil**
½ tsp **chilli flakes**
Pinch of **pepper**

THE FAR EASTERN RUB

The spices and herbs of the Far East seem to be made for waterfowl. They bring out and balance the rich depth of flavour in the meat. This rub is simple but gives any avian dish an oriental twist.

This rub is especially good on many East-Asian-style duck dishes.

Using a mortar and pestle, grind all the ingredients together to create a medium-to-fine consistency. And you're done!

Use on waterfowl and upland birds.

5 minutes

 Makes 10g

½ tsp **dried thyme**
½ tsp **dried rosemary**
½ tsp **garlic powder**
½ tsp **smoked paprika**
½ tsp **coarse gourmet peppercorns**
¼ tsp **lemon pepper**

UP YOUR GAME PEPPER STEAK SEASONING

Quick and easy. This lightweight, packable and easy-to-store seasoning is a great addition to your back country experience.

Mix all the ingredients together in a small bowl and store in an airtight container.

Use this beautiful seasoning to enhance your upland game bird.

Store in a cool dry container for up to 6 months.

 5 minutes

 Makes 500g

1 tsp finely chopped **rosemary leaves**
1 tsp finely chopped **chives**
1 tsp finely chopped **flat-leaf parsley**
1 tsp finely chopped **thyme** (only use stalks if soft; otherwise, use the leaves and flowers)
1 tsp finely chopped **sage**
2–3 cloves **garlic**, finely chopped
500g **butter**

HERB BUTTER

I just love this herb butter and use it all the time. Trust me, I always have it on me – and when you taste it, you will too!

In a bowl, combine the chopped herbs and garlic.

Soften the butter and add it to the bowl. Using a spatula, fold the herbs through the butter, mixing thoroughly until combined.

Refrigerate in an airtight jar or container for up to 30 days or freeze for up to 6 months.

WATERFOWL

MALLARD/GREY · PARADISE SHELDUCK · SHOVELER DUCK · PUKEKO · BLACK SWAN

The mallard is the most common duck in New Zealand, where it was introduced, and also in the Northern Hemisphere, where it originally comes from.

From 1867 repeated attempts were made by acclimatisation societies to introduce British-sourced mallards into New Zealand. However, their success was initially somewhat localised. With some notable exceptions, over much of the country they remained rare or unknown.

Major John Whitney and later his son Sir Cecil Whitney, both of the Colonial Ammunition Company (C.A.C.), persisted with these imports, often at their own expense, initially obtaining birds from England in 1886, 1910 and 1912 through close family connections. Then in 1914, Sir Cecil imported 600 more mallards from Scotland where, as a lad, he had helped the gamekeeper raise and release mallards on his father's sporting lease at Knockbrex. Later, in the 1930s and '40s, in his ongoing quest for 'pure' mallards, Sir Cecil obtained further mallards from America with the help of Ducks Unlimited connections. These birds were brought over initially as deck passengers on ocean liners from San Francisco, but he later imported them as eggs, probably as air freight on early flying boats.

Sir Cecil raised many birds from these imports and for decades shared their progeny, birds and eggs, with acclimatisation societies and interested individuals the length of the country, sometimes including imported partridges and pheasants as well. This activity increased, especially in the 1930s and '40s, driven by the collapse of the native grey duck, which simply couldn't cope with the industrial scale drainage of wetlands. A massive 90% of wetlands in New Zealand were lost, far more than in the USA, for instance. Closed seasons for the grey duck were regularly proposed and sometimes enacted, for example, in 1942. It wasn't until around the 1960s that the mallard, much more adaptable to a modified environment, started breaking out from its few bridgeheads around the country, and began occupying the much-modified landscape that the grey duck had left vacant. From there, it never looked back, and today millions

of mallards are the mainstay of our duck hunting in New Zealand. The grey duck continues to hang on wherever large-scale natural wetlands remain protected from drainage.

Mallards are most likely found on shallow freshwater bodies such as wetlands and ponds, lakes and even flooded fields.

They are a medium-to-large dabbling duck that is most recognisable by the male's glossy green head and white collar around the neck.

The female is a mottled brown with a brown bill.

Both sexes have orange feet and a purple-blue speculum with both sides outlined in white.

PREPARATION:

With any game, it is essential to allow the birds to cool quickly with air circulating around them. Therefore, many hunters hang them in pairs ('braced up'), with a strip of flax wrapped through their nostrils, under the bill and then back under itself (so no knot required). They then hang these on a nail on the shady side of the maimai.

Hunters often breast the birds as this contains most of the usable meat. However, the drumsticks have their uses too. Or you can pluck and roast the whole bird, especially nice fat drakes.

Beware that recipes for farmyard ducks, while they are a helpful guide for ingredient choice, are almost for a different bird. Farmyard ducks are very fatty, whereas wild mallards are much more heart-healthy, very lean meat. You will need to be very careful not to dry the latter out. Do not, for instance, prick the breast all over to let the fat out. There isn't any! Wrapping foil over the roasting dish until perhaps 20 minutes before they are done (to then crisp and brown up the skin) will help keep the roast bird moist. Next, check with a sharp knife cut made to the skin between the breast and the leg; open the cut just enough to see if the juices at the base of the inner leg are red, pink, clear or dry. Red or dark pink, keep cooking. Clear is ideal. If dry, remove it from the oven immediately.

If you stuff the bird, you can truss up the vent hole using simple stainless-steel trussing needles from a cookery shop. Weave some brown string around these, similar to lacing up boots and tying them off. This will keep your stuffing in. Remove the string and needles when the bird is done. One lady who lived much of her life in the north of Scotland explained that wild duck was regularly on the menu, but its taste would be quite different each time depending on whatever fruit it was stuffed with, so they never got bored with it.

Wild duck is delicious cold the next day for lunch too. So why not be the envy of your workmates. Better still, invite them along with you next time.

Wild rice is a traditional accompaniment to many American recipes and is now much easier to buy in New Zealand. Or serve with red cabbage or Brussel sprouts, parsley potatoes and a nice sauce to make a mighty fine meal to help relive and celebrate your day in the field.

– John Dyer, Fish & Game New Zealand

SAGE MALLARD WITH ROAST CAULIFLOWER

Roast duck with a Middle-Eastern twist! Coming from Cyprus originally, with a Cypriot Dad, the flavours of the Middle East were often fused into my mother's Italian recipes. I grew up with a love of both, and often combine my favourite flavours of both cultures in the dishes I create. This one is a great example of a flavourful fusion.

RUB
Rub-A-Dub Duckie Rub
(see page 37)

BIRD
1 **whole duck**
1 **large oven bag**
1 clove **garlic**, crushed
Knob of **butter**
½ **chilli**, sliced

SAGE LEAVES
Knob of **butter**
16 **sage leaves**

SIDE
½ head of **cauliflower**, de-stemmed
4 **baby onions**, halved
1 Tbsp **olive oil**
1 tsp **truffle oil**
1 tsp **fig balsamic vinegar**
Salt & pepper

TO SERVE
Angelo's Famous Tzatziki Sauce (see page 33)
1 Tbsp **black tahini**

Preheat the oven to 160°C.

Cover the whole duck with the rub.

Place the duck along with the crushed garlic, a knob of butter and the sliced chilli into a large oven bag. Pierce a small hole in the oven bag to release the steam, tie up and place in the oven for 3 hours.

In a hot frying pan with a knob of butter, fry the sage leaves for 3-5 minutes or until crispy. Using tongs, carefully remove the leaves from the pan.

Place the cauliflower and baby onions in an oven dish. Drizzle with the olive oil, truffle oil and the fig balsamic vinegar and season with salt and pepper. Place in the oven for 45 minutes or until golden and soft, timing it so the duck and cauliflower are finished cooking at the same time.

Serve with a dollop of tzatziki sauce and a drizzle of black tahini over the cauliflower.

BLACK PLUM & TOMATO MALLARD CASSEROLE

Who doesn't love their slow cooker? A seriously brilliant invention for creating classic, warm-the-cockles-of-your-heart casseroles that you can set and forget. Coming home to the rich aroma of plums, tomatoes, and melt-in-your-mouth duck? Man, oh man, is it winter yet?

4 Tbsp **olive oil**

10 small **pickling onions**

6 **duck legs**

4 cloves **garlic** , crushed

Salt & **pepper**

1 x 680g bottle **tomato passata**

1 Tbsp **wholegrain mustard**

¼ cup **red wine**

3 sprigs **fresh thyme**, roughly chopped

2 sprigs **fresh rosemary**, roughly chopped

1 **bay leaf**

½ handful of **fresh parsley**, roughly chopped

1 **lemon**, wedged

1 Tbsp **balsamic vinegar**

½ tsp **ground cinnamon**

6 **fresh** or **tinned black plums**, halved and destoned

Turn your slow cooker to auto or medium.

In a large hot frying pan, brown the pickling onions in olive oil. Next add the duck legs and brown both sides. Add the garlic and season with salt and pepper. Transfer into the slow cooker.

Add the remaining ingredients (except the plums) into the slow cooker and turn to low. Simmer for 4 hours. After 3 hours, add the 6 black plums skin-side down and simmer for a further 1 hour.

Season to taste and serve.

TIP: If you use tinned plums, place them into the slow cooker 30 minutes before the 4 hours is up, as the plums will go mushy if left in the cooker for too long.

MALLARD CONFIT WITH ROAST QUINCE & RED WINE JUS

I love quince! It's such a versatile fruit and makes the best darn jelly ever. Combined here with succulent roast mallard and my rich Red Wine Jus, this is a hearty meal heavy on flavour. It may take some time to cook but it's two for one! The beautifully infused duck fat can be set aside to use in future recipes.

BIRD

4-6 **mallard legs**

½ cup **coarse sea salt**

Handful of **thyme**, chopped

2 **bay leaves**

2 pinches of **nutmeg**

QUINCE

2 **quince**

100g **butter**

2 **bay leaves**

2 cloves **garlic**, crushed

2 **shallots**, halved

8 Tbsp **duck fat**

TO SERVE

Red Wine Jus (see page 36)

Place the duck legs into a bowl, add coarse sea salt, thyme, bay leaves, nutmeg and toss the ingredients together to ensure the meat is covered.

Place in the fridge for 24 hours. This will give the meat a nice texture.

After 24 hours, rinse the duck legs with water to remove the salt and pat dry with paper towels.

Preheat the oven to 140°C.

In a deep hot oven-proof frying pan add 50g of butter and brown the duck legs for about 5 minutes or until golden brown on both sides. Add the quince to the hot pan with another 50g of butter, and put 1 bay leaf, a clove of crushed garlic and a shallot on top of each quince. Now add the duck fat to the pan, checking the duck legs are submerged, and place the pan in the oven for 2 hours or until the meat is tender.

Once cooked, remove from the fat and serve the duck legs and quince with a red wine jus.

TIP: Confit means to cook something 'low & slow' submerged in fat or oil. This method of cooking requires the meat to be salted as part of the preservation process before cooking it, so don't skip this part!

ROAST MALLARD & MARMALADE

Duck and oranges go together like peas and carrots! This is my tasty twist on duck à l'orange, a classic French dish that I've given a tangy tune-up.

BIRD

1 **whole mallard duck**
Salt & **pepper**
1 Tbsp **duck fat**
100g **butter**
1 **oven bag**
¾ cup **orange juice**

MARMALADE

1 **whole orange**, peel and juice
2 cloves **garlic**, minced
½ **onion**, sliced
¼ cup **orange juice**
6 Tbsp **brown sugar**
1 Tbsp **runny honey**
½ tsp **allspice**
1 Tbsp **balsamic glaze**

TO SERVE

¼ cup **whole almonds**
¼ cup **sliced almonds**
½ Tbsp **honey**
Dehydrated orange slices
(optional)

Preheat oven to 160°C.

Pat the duck dry using paper towels and season it with salt and pepper.

In a large hot pan add the duck fat and butter, and brown the duck, covering all sides.

Place the duck in an oven bag, carefully pouring in the hot juices from the pan and adding the orange juice. Tie and pierce the bag and place in the oven for 2 hours.

Turn off the oven and let the bird rest in the oven for a further 30 minutes.

While the bird is resting, make the marmalade. Using a potato peeler, carefully peel the skin off the orange, leaving as much of the white flesh behind as possible (as it can taste bitter). Using a sharp knife, slice the peel into thin strips. Put the peel into a large saucepan and add the juice from the orange along with the rest of the marmalade ingredients and mix together. Simmer the marmalade mixture for 30 minutes or until thickened. Stir in the balsamic glaze and set aside to cool.

To toast the almonds: In a hot pan, add the whole and sliced almonds and toast until golden brown. Turn down the heat to low, then add the honey to the pan and stir ensuring the almonds are covered, being careful not to burn them. Once the almonds are honey glazed, remove from heat.

To serve, pour the marmalade over the duck and sprinkle with the almonds. Decorate with dehydrated oranges slices.

MALLARD & TAMARILLO WITH SWEET SOY SAUCE

Inspired by my travels, this is a bit of a fun fusion of Asian flavours that makes this duck dish a taste explosion. Tamarillo is a winter fruit here in New Zealand. If you can't get your hands on fresh tamarillos, tamarillo chutney or sauce will work as well.

DUCK
2 **mallard duck legs**
2 Tbsp **duck fat**

RUB
The Far Eastern Rub
(see page 38)

SAUCE
2 cloves **garlic**, chopped
4 **tamarillos**, roughly chopped
½ **red onion**, sliced
½ **red chilli**, sliced
½ thumb of **ginger**
Pinch of **Chinese five spice**
¾ cup **orange juice**
1 Tbsp **sesame oil**
1 Tbsp **duck fat**
4 Tbsp **sweet soy sauce**
2 Tbsp **caster sugar**

TO SERVE
Handful of **fresh coriander leaves**, roughly chopped
1 tsp **white sesame seeds**

Preheat the oven to 200°C.

In a hot saucepan add all the sauce ingredients and stir together, reduce the heat and simmer for 15-20 minutes or until thickened.

Coat the duck legs with the rub.

On a hot skillet or deep frying pan add the duck fat.

Place the duck legs into the pan and brown for approx. 3 minutes on each side or until the rub is golden brown.

Pour sauce over the duck legs. Place in the oven for 20 minutes. Remove from the oven and let rest for 10 minutes.

Garnish with coriander and sesame seeds.

CRISPY MALLARD PANCAKES

Finger licking goodness! These crispy duck pancakes are a little bit of bite-sized heaven! For best results I recommend using a bamboo steamer. You can find these at any Asian supermarket and they are really handy to have on hand in the kitchen!

DUCK

2 **mallard legs**

2 **mallard breasts**

450g **duck fat**

½ tsp **sesame seed oil**

1 Tbsp **sweet soy sauce** (GF optional)

PANCAKES

1 **egg**

1 cup **flour** (GF optional)

1 cup **milk**

2 pinches **salt**

25g **butter**

TO SERVE

1 Tbsp **Cranberry & Prune BBQ Sauce** (see page 28)

1 **spring onion**, sliced

¼ **cucumber**, sliced

1 tsp **tamari roasted sunflower seeds**

In a bamboo (or conventional) steamer, place the duck legs onto the bottom shelf and the breasts on the top shelf. Steam the duck for 1 hour. Don't forget to top up the water as it evaporates.

Into a deep hot frying pan, add your duck fat. Once the fat has reached frying temperature (180°C), carefully place the duck legs and breasts into the frying pan using tongs. Deep fry for 10 minutes. Carefully remove the duck from the hot fat, placing it into a bowl. Lightly drizzle sesame seed oil and sweet soy sauce over the duck. Once cooled, shred the meat off the legs and breasts using two forks, being mindful to avoid sharp leg bones.

To make the pancakes, whisk egg, flour and milk together for 5-10 minutes to get as much air into the mixture as possible. If needed, add extra milk one tablespoon at a time until a silky, runny consistency is achieved. Add salt to finish the batter. In a warm frying pan, melt a knob of butter and add 3 Tbsp of the pancake batter to make 1 pancake. Use the back of the spoon to form a pancake shape. Cook for 3 minutes on both sides.

To assemble the pancake; spread BBQ sauce over the base, place spring onions, cucumber and sunflower seeds in the centre. Place the deep fried duck on top with a drizzle more BBQ sauce.

Fold pancake and place into mouth.

MALLARD PIE

Hearty, wholesome, and wholly scrumptious – Kiwis love a good pie. I give you – duck pie! I'm pretty excited for you to try this pie for yourself. It's so good, I can't even describe it! You won't want to share so make sure you make enough for everyone! 1 breast per pie.

DUCK

4 **mallard breasts**, precooked

Salt & **pepper**

2 Tbsp **duck fat**

50g **butter**

1 **bay leaf**

4 sprigs **thyme**

1 Tbsp **maple syrup** (or runny honey)

PASTRY

A **deep dish** or 4 **pie tins**

Cooking oil spray for greasing

Pre-made puff pastry (GF Optional)

FILLING

2 Tbsp **olive oil**

2 cloves **garlic**, halved

1 **white onion**, sliced

2 **zucchini**, shaved

3 pinches of **salt**

3 pinches of **pepper**

1 tsp **white truffle oil**

1 tsp **dried mixed herbs** or 1 handful of **fresh herbs**, chopped

1 **chicken stock cube**

1 cup **thickened cream**

12 **cherry tomatoes**

1 **egg yolk**

Preheat oven to 160°C

In a hot pan with duck fat, season the duck breasts and brown on both sides.

Place the duck breasts into an oven bag adding the butter, bay leaf, thyme and syrup. Place into the oven for 1 hour 45 minutes. Take out and let it rest for a further 30mins.

When it's cooled, turn the oven up to 180°C.

Take the pie dish/tins and spray with cooking oil. Add the puff pastry into the dish/tins with the edges of the pastry overhanging the sides.

For the pie mixture, in a hot deep frying pan, use olive oil to brown the garlic, onion, zucchini, salt, pepper, white truffle oil, herbs and the stock cube. Add the cream and stir until mixture has thickened. Take off the heat to cool.

Once cooled, spoon the filling mixture into the pie dish/tins. Cut the duck breasts into slices and place them on top of each pie with 3 cherry tomatoes. Brush the edges of the pastry with egg yolk and place in oven for 20 minutes or until pastry is golden brown.

Serve with your favourite chutney, or peas, mash and gravy.

TIP: all ingredients need to be cooled or at room temperature before placing into the pastry otherwise the pastry will have a soggy bottom.

PARADISE SHELDUCK

Paradise ducks or 'parries' are a New Zealand conservation success story.

The paradise duck is New Zealand's only shelduck, which means it is a rather gooselike duck.

When Pākehā first settled the country, our native paradise duck was rare and absent over large parts of New Zealand.

The conversion of bush to pasture, topdressing, and the creation of many stock ponds (thousands of which were subsidised by hunters' licence fees) caused their numbers to explode.

Their spread was helped by the Wildlife Service, assisted by acclimatisation societies, relocating birds from the few concentrations of birds left into other regions around the 1960s.

Unusually for ducks, the female paradise shelduck is more eye-catching than the male; females have a pure white head and chestnut-coloured body, while males have a dark grey body and black head.

Parries are very vocal birds, with males giving a characteristic 'zonk zonk', while females make a more shrill 'zeek zeek' while flying or as a warning to intruders.

HUNTING:

Paradise shelducks are commonly observed in pairs, usually holding a breeding territory, or in flocks of younger pre-breeding age birds (usually 1-2 years old). Hunters tend to target the younger flocks.

Hunting breaks up larger flocks into smaller groups that farmers find more acceptable. This is especially so in drought time when farmers are short of feed. This is why many Fish & Game regions with more significant numbers of paradise shelducks have special summer dispersal seasons when their carefully monitored populations of parries can sustain the extra harvest.

Parries can often be stalked. Resist the temptation to stand up and look as you approach. Instead, pick a tall object and work your way in close, remaining down and out of sight.

Silhouette decoys are very useful to put birds in range. These can be shop-purchased or homemade from plywood and then suitably painted. If you have found a spot in a paddock where the parries have been feeding, as evidenced by poo and feathers on the ground and perhaps also the birds you flushed off, then set up quick. Keep out of sight, under a camo net or camouflaged next to a fence line or bushes, and keep close to your decoys. If you have found a mounting pond, this is another top spot to hunt.

The first birds brought down can be used as decoys in the field or beside the pond to get the attention of other birds trading past, or use your silhouettes or floaters, as appropriate. Face them into the wind. Special parry calls are available on the market (both mouth-blown and electronic) and work to get passing birds' attention.

Resist the temptation to sneak up and blaze away at 100 or more birds. Instead, flush them off, and get ready quickly for them to come back in dribs and drabs. You'll usually have a much heavier bag for being patient. If the opening morning action goes quiet in your district, wait a bit for other hunters to think the same and start wandering about disturbing small flocks. If you're still beside your decoys, you'll soon benefit from their activity. Or send one of your party off to do the disturbing.

Contrary to what you might think, these large birds seem no harder to kill than mallards, so your standard duck load in standard shot sizes should do just fine.

Experienced hunters aim for the drakes, which have more meat.

PREPARATION:

Plucking parries is quite a bit harder than for smaller dabbling ducks like mallards and greys. So most hunters breast them instead. Many hunters nowadays take this and other game meat they've saved up to a licenced game butcher who turns it into sausages and salamis. Just phone ahead to make sure your butcher is one of those that have the correct permits to do this. It will help significantly if you make every effort to remove any steel shot pellets as these can damage the butcher's blades.

Be sure to take a spade and bury any feathers or carcasses leftover rather than leave an eyesore for the farmer to find. It's a good idea to ask in advance if there's anywhere special he wants you to bury this material, as you don't want to discover his main waterpipe accidentally.

Often in the summer parry seasons, there are still swimming moulters on ponds – birds that have not yet regained their flight feathers. Moulting requires a lot of energy, and moulters are usually in poor condition with not much meat. We recommended that you leave them be for another hunter in the future.

Parry meat is a little coarser than mallard, but three things will make it hard for anyone to tell them apart, even served side by side on a dinner plate. One: target the flocks. These younger birds will typically be better to eat, especially roasted, although, with care, even much older birds (up to 12 years old!) will still make good meals if stewed or casseroled. Two: don't leave the birds you shot in the field as decoys in the sun all day, or their meat will spoil. If you must do this on a hot day, we suggest you breast them first and leave their meat in the shade of a tree with some fly-proof muslin cloth covering it. Lastly, this applies to all game birds, don't overcook it and dry it out, or it will be much tougher (how to avoid this has been described in the mallard section).

– John Dyer, Fish & Game New Zealand

WHOLESOME & HEARTY PARADISE SHELDUCK DISH

A staple for the maimai. Nutritious and 'hearty'– pardon the pun! – this is a quick and easy recipe to warm you up after a long, wet day. I also love not wasting any part of the bird, so this recipe gets a thumbs up from me! It's also high in iron and protein to keep a hungry hunter full and energised.

SAUCE

½ Tbsp **cooking oil**

Knob of **butter**

6 small **pickling onions**, halved

5 **field mushrooms**, sliced

3 sprigs **thyme leaves**

½ cup **cream**

BIRD

Knob of **butter**

2 Tbsp **olive oil**

2 cloves **garlic**, sliced

1 rasher **bacon**, chopped

6 **paradise duck hearts**

6 **paradise duck livers**

Salt & **pepper**

In a hot frying pan, brown the onions and mushrooms in the cooking oil and butter. Add the thyme and cream. Lower the heat and simmer for 12-15 minutes or until thickened, stirring regularly.

In another hot frying pan add a knob of butter and the olive oil, and brown the bacon and garlic. Add the duck livers and hearts, and continue to brown for another 5-10 minutes.

Add the sauce to the duck hearts and livers. Stir regularly until the sauce has turned a golden brown colour.

Season to taste and serve.

SWEET & STICKY PARADISE SHELDUCK LEGS WITH CHERRY SAUCE

Six legs are better than two! And these roast duck legs are so good you'll want them all for yourself! The pomegranate molasses gives this dish a tangy sweetness and is super high in antioxidants and vitamin C, so even though it tastes decadent, it's good for you!

BIRD

6 **paradise duck legs**

1 **oven bag**

50g **butter**

3 pinches of **salt**

3 pinches of **pepper**

1 tsp **pomegranate molasses**

1 clove **garlic**, halved

1 sprig **thyme**

1 sprig **rosemary**

CARROTS

400g **gourmet carrots**, halved lengthways

Salt & **pepper**

1 Tbsp **olive oil**

1 tsp **pomegranate molasses**

1 Tbsp **runny honey**

4 cloves **garlic**, crushed

SAUCE

Knob of **butter**

2 Tbsp **pomegranate molasses**

Salt & **pepper**

TO SERVE

Cherry Brandy Sauce
(see page 29)

Preheat the oven to 160°C.

Place the duck legs in an oven bag along with the butter, salt and pepper, pomegranate molasses, garlic, thyme and rosemary. Tie up the bag and shake. Pierce the bag and place in the oven for 3 hours or until legs are tender.

A short while before the duck is ready, start preparing the carrots. Season and oil a roasting dish, add the carrots and drizzle over the olive oil, pomegranate molasses and honey. Add the garlic and season again. Place the carrots in the oven with the duck for 30 minutes. Your carrots and duck should be ready at the same time.

For the sauce, place a saucepan over a low heat and melt the butter. Add the pomegranate molasses and season with salt and pepper. Stir well.

Pour the pomegranate sauce over the carrots and duck, and serve with warm Cherry Brandy Sauce.

PEACHY KEEN PARADISE SHELDUCK

Simple yet sumptuous, these stuffed paradise duck breasts are juicy, tasty, really easy to make and make a meal fit for a king!

BIRD

2 **paradise duck breasts**

Salt & **pepper**

1 Tbsp **cooking oil**

STUFFING

Knob of **butter**

1 tsp **duck fat**

425g **tin peaches**

½ Tbsp **brown sugar**

¼ tsp **cinnamon**

1 clove **garlic**, finely sliced

TO SERVE

Roast peaches

Cherry tomatoes

Preheat the oven to 180°C.

Season the duck breasts on both sides with salt and pepper.

In a hot frying pan, heat the oil and brown the duck skin-side down. Take off the heat and set aside to cool.

In a hot pan, add a knob of butter with the duck fat. Add the drained peaches to the pan and sprinkle with brown sugar and cinnamon. Add the garlic and caramelise the peaches on both sides. Take off the heat and set aside to cool. Save a handful of peaches for your side.

Carefully make an incision between the duck breast flesh and skin, creating a flap. Stuff your peach mixture under the flap and place in the oven for 20 minutes. Once cooked, remove from the oven and let the bird rest for 10 minutes.

At the same time, place the remaining cooked peaches on a separate tray in the oven and roast for 30 minutes.

Enjoy your roast peaches and Peachy Keen Paradise Shelduck garnished with cherry tomatoes.

PAN-FRIED PARADISE SHELDUCK WITH BRUSSEL SPROUTS, BLUE CHEESE & ROAST BEETROOT SALAD

Decadent paradise duck breast done well is a dinner time showstopper. It might all sound fancy, but you'll be surprised at how easy this dish is to make and how incredible it tastes. All the flavours come together to create a perfect match – you could even say a match made in paradise! (Yes, I had to!)

RUB

Rub-A-Dub Duckie Rub
(see page 37)

DUCK

Knob of **butter**

250g **paradise duck breasts**
(2 breasts)

1 **whole beetroot**, sliced into wedges

SAUCE

3 Tbsp **Blackberry & Port Sauce** (see page 28)

SALAD

10 **Brussel sprouts**

Knob of **garlic butter**

Salt & **pepper**

100g **blue cheese**, cubed

1 Tbsp **sweetcorn**

SIDE

Bunch of **black** or **red grapes**

3 Tbsp **balsamic vinegar**

Salt & **pepper**

Preheat the oven to 180°C.

Cover the duck breasts with the rub.

In a hot frying pan, add a knob of butter and brown the duck skin-side down along with the beetroot wedges. Once the duck skin is golden brown, turn over and place into the oven for 15 minutes.

Once the bird is cooked, set aside to rest. Leave the beetroot in the oven, adding the grapes, and drizzle the balsamic vinegar with a pinch of salt and pepper over the top. Cook in the oven for a further 15 minutes or until softened. Set aside.

In a hot saucepan, take the juices from the rested duck breasts, add the Blackberry & Port Sauce, and simmer for 5 minutes or until thickened.

To prepare the Brussel sprouts, peel away the outer leaves (reserve these), cut the sprouts in half and trim off the stalks. In a hot pan with a knob of garlic butter, brown the Brussel sprouts, until they are dark brown in colour but not burnt! This should take about 10 minutes. Salt and pepper to taste. Remove from heat and set aside.

Once the Brussel sprouts have reached room temperature, put them into a bowl and toss them together with the peeled leaves, blue cheese, sweetcorn and the roast beetroot.

To serve, cut the duck breasts into slices. Drizzle the Blackberry & Port Sauce over the bird, accompany with grapes and salad. Delicious.

SPICED LIME CURRY WITH PARADISE SHELDUCK

Originating in China, the persimmon is a delicately flavoured orange fruit with velvety flesh much like an apricot. The sweetness balances the zesty spices of the curry perfectly. However, if persimmons are out of season or you can't get hold of them, mangoes make for a nice alternative.

BIRD

250g **paradise duck breasts** (2 breasts)

Salt & **pepper**

Pinch of **ground coriander seeds**

Pinch of **ground ginger**

Pinch of **ground Chinese five spice**

Zest and **juice** of 1 **lime**

½ Tbsp **duck fat**

¼ tsp **sweet soy sauce**

CURRY SAUCE

Knob of **butter**

3 **persimmons**, cubed, skin on

½ cup **orange juice**

½ cup **white wine**

1 clove **garlic**, chopped

¼ **red chilli**, deseeded and sliced

3 pinches of **saffron**

160ml **coconut milk**

3 pinches of **turmeric**

3 pinches of **smoked paprika**

TO SERVE

Wild rice, cooked

1 Tbsp **fresh coriander leaves**

Preheat the oven to 200°C.

In a bowl season the duck breasts with salt and pepper and add the coriander, ginger and Chinese five spice. Squeeze the lime juice and zest over the duck. Allow the duck breasts to marinate in the lime juice for 10 minutes.

In a hot frying pan, add the duck fat and place the breasts skin-side down. Add the soy sauce and brown on both sides until the skin has turned crispy. Place into the oven for 15 minutes.

In a hot saucepan, place a knob of butter and add the persimmons. Allow to cook until softened. Turn the heat down to a simmer. Add the orange juice, white wine, garlic, red chilli, saffron, coconut milk, turmeric and smoked paprika. Stir occasionally and cook for 12-15 minutes or until thickened.

Once the duck breasts are cooked, let them rest for 5 minutes and then slice.

Serve with the curry sauce, wild rice and a sprinkle of coriander leaves on top.

TIP: wash the rice with cold water before boiling to remove the starch.

MAIMAI SOUVLAKI

Nothing beats a pocket of tasty goodness! with my Cypriot Greek heritage, you know I love a good Souvlaki, and this tasty hunter's snack is lip-smackingly good. No cutlery needed!

TZATZIKI SAUCE
Angelo's Famous Tzatziki Sauce (see page 33)

SALAD
½ **small red onion**, sliced
Small handful of **coriander leaves**, chopped
2 **medium tomatoes**, chopped
¼ **cucumber**, sliced
6 **feta cubes** (half a 200g packet)

SKEWERS
2 **duck breasts**, 3cm cubes
1 **red capsicum**, 2cm pieces
Pinch of **smoked paprika**
Pinch of **turmeric**
Pinch of **cumin**
Salt & **pepper**

TO SERVE
Pita bread
Lemon juice
1 tsp **olive oil**

Prepare the salad by lightly tossing all the ingredients together. Set aside.

Skewer the duck breasts and capsicum, alternating between the two. Place the skewers on the BBQ and cook to your liking, turning the skewers to cook the meat evenly. Sprinkle the skewers with paprika, turmeric, cumin, salt and pepper.

Lightly brush some olive oil over the pita bread and warm it on the BBQ.

Now to put these beauties together. Carefully slice an opening into the warm pita pocket. Add the tzatziki, the salad and the meat and capsicum which have been removed from the skewers. Squeeze some lemon juice on top and finally add a dollop of tzatziki sauce to finish.

Devour within minutes!

SHOVELER

As long as there has been recreational game bird shooting in New Zealand (which started incidentally with the crew of Captain Cook's Endeavour), the shoveler duck has been a special prize.

This bird, also known as the 'spoonie', was ironically less common last century, but there are now around 150,000 in New Zealand.

The spoonie has comb-like openings in the side of its spoon-shaped bill (hence its name) that let it sift fine insect life from the surface of biologically rich wetlands.

Because of its specialised habits, it is unlikely ever to be very common, but birds have moved into wetlands designed for them by Fish & Game New Zealand.

The male shoveler is New Zealand's most handsome duck, with variegated plumage, blue-grey head with a white vertical stripe between the eye and bill, a striking reddish-brown breast, and blue wings.

The female is more plainly embellished with cryptic brown similar to female mallards and grey ducks.

This is nature's way of providing camouflage when she is nesting and brood-rearing.

Drakes also go through an eclipse moult (like mallard drakes), which means that you will find them at certain times of the year in various stages between looking like hen spoonies and sporting their full drake plumage. The more cryptic colouring allows them to moult (a summer flightless period that will enable them to regrow their flight feathers) without attracting undue attention from hawks and so on.

This species is one of the hardest waterfowl to band. However, when we have had subsequent hunter-recoveries, it's clear this is one of our most wide-ranging game ducks, often flying the length of New Zealand. Interestingly, female shovelers have been found nesting just metres away from where they were nesting the previous year.

HUNTING:

In certain waterfowl species, drakes outnumber their female ducks. We know from the nationwide annual trend-count survey of this species by Fish & Game staff and volunteers that this is especially so with the shoveler in New Zealand. There are more than two drakes for every hen bird. For this reason, we recommend hunters 'go for blue'; in other words, pick out the more colourful drake, which is surplus to the number of pairs required in this species.

A spoonie is a prize for another reason; it is also our fastest game bird. When they first whoosh past the decoys, the lead you need to give them (the distance you shoot in front of them to connect) seems several times more than any other wild duck. But once they land and take off, their speed is much more conventional.

Spoonies also make a great-looking taxidermy mount, either the drake on his own or a pair together.

PREPARATION:

What applies to mallards and greys also applies to spoonies, of course, because they are all similar 'dabbling duck' species. However, the shoveler is a smaller bird that, when roasted, is typically a fine meal for just one person.

– John Dyer, Fish & Game New Zealand

HERBS & HONEY ROAST SHOVELER WITH DUCK FAT POTATOES

A huge part of what I do with my wild kitchen philosophy is to use as much of the game as possible. With duck, any kind of duck, nearly every part of it can be utilised. This is what I see as honouring the bird, giving thanks for the sustenance it offers. And the fat makes the most deliciously crisp and tasty potatoes!

BIRD

1 **whole shoveler**

1 **large oven bag**

2 rashers **bacon**

7 **sage leaves**

½ **white onion**, sliced

3 cloves **garlic**, crushed

1 Tbsp **runny honey**

Knob of **butter**

Salt & **pepper**

POTATOES

2 **agria potatoes**, diced into 2.5cm cubes

Up to 800g **duck fat**

SAUCE

Cherry Brandy Sauce
(see page 29)

Preheat oven to 155°C.

Place into the oven bag the shoveler, bacon, sage, sliced onion, crushed garlic, runny honey, butter and pinch of seasoning. Tie and pierce the oven bag and place in the oven for 2 hours 45 minutes.

For the roast potatoes, bring some water to the boil in a saucepan and add the potatoes, cooking for 8-10 minutes until the potatoes are parboiled. Drain and leave to sit for a few minutes to allow the water residue to evaporate.

Take a deep pan, place on a high heat and add the duck fat and heat until the fat is very hot. To test this, place one potato cube in the pan, if it sizzles it's hot enough and good to go. Make sure you add enough duck fat to completely cover the potatoes. Carefully add the potato cubes, and deep fry for approx. 5 minutes or until golden brown.

Remove the potatoes from the hot fat by using a skimming ladle or perforated spoon and place on paper towels to absorb any remaining fat.

Drizzle the Cherry Brandy Sauce over the bird and serve with the duck fat roast potatoes.

TIP: To tell if your potatoes are parboiled, insert a fork into one. The fork should slide in easily, meeting some resistance in the centre.

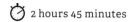
HONEY SOY ROAST SHOVELER WITH BLACKBERRY & PLUM SAUCE & PAN-SEARED PEARS

Healthy, light, delicious and easy, this is a no-fuss meal that everyone will enjoy! The sweet flavours will make it a family fave!

DUCK

1 **whole shoveler**

1 **large oven bag**

25g **butter**

2 cloves **garlic**, crushed

1 Tbsp **sweet soy sauce**

1 Tbsp **runny honey**

PEAR

1 **red pear**, halved

1 tsp **butter**

SAUCE

Blackberry & Plum Sauce (see page 29)

TO SERVE

2 handfuls of **mesclun salad**

½ handful of **mint leaves**, sliced

½ Tbsp **avocado oil**

1 Tbsp **balsamic vinegar**

Salt & **pepper**

Preheat oven to 160°C.

In an oven bag, add the shoveler, butter, crushed garlic, sweet soy sauce and runny honey. Pierce and tie the bag and carefully shake to coat the bird. Place in the oven for 2 hours 30 minutes.

In a hot frying pan, add the butter and place the pear flesh-side down and fry for 1-2 minutes or until golden brown. Set aside.

Warm up your Blackberry & Plum Sauce using a hot pan or microwave.

Serve with tossed mesclun salad and mint leaves. Drizzle avocado oil and balsamic vinegar over the salad with added salt and pepper to taste.

A beautiful light dish of shoveler and pear with a side salad.

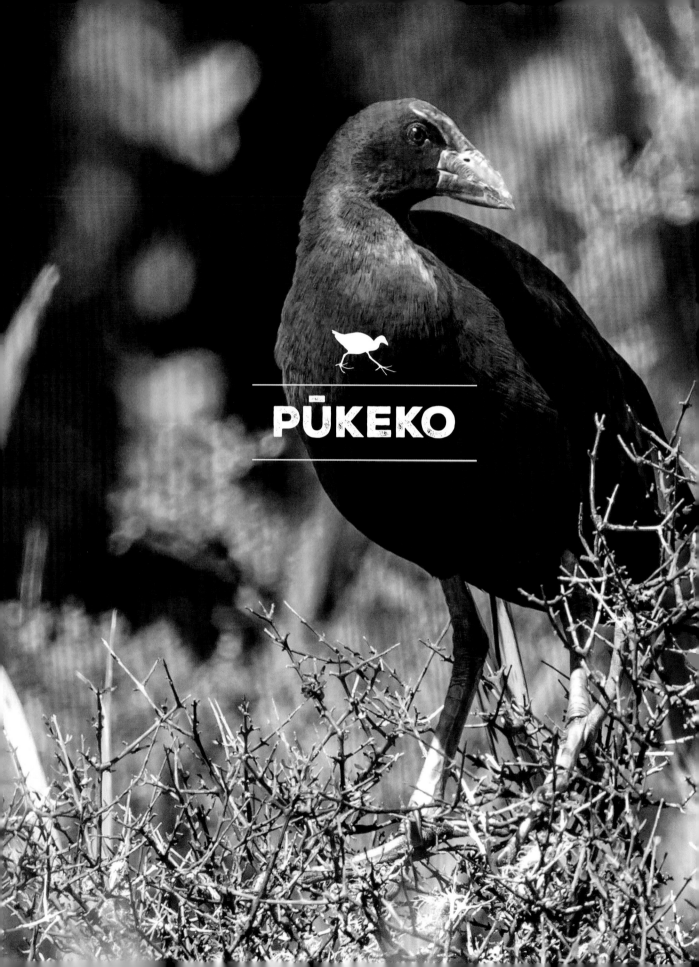

PŪKEKO

Often the subject of myth and delight, the pūkeko is a wonderful game bird to eat.

The New Zealand pūkeko (*Porphyrio melanotus*) is a large, blue-purplish, wetland-dwelling bird.

Pūkeko are held in mixed affection by New Zealanders; they are very territorial and have a reputation as friendly, cheeky birds.

Often called the 'swamp hen', 'pook', or to some hunters, the 'blue pheasant'.

The pūkeko is a member of the rail family of birds and are found in northern and eastern Australia, Tasmania and New Zealand, including the Kermadec and Chatham Islands.

They have benefited from land clearance and development for pasture, crops, and market gardening like paradise shelduck and the Canada goose.

They have also adapted well to urbanisation.

PŪKEKO BEHAVIOUR

The pūkeko is a great wader and runner.

When disturbed, they much prefer to run or hide than to fly.

However, when pushed, they are strong fliers and can fly long distances if needed. They're sometimes seen on the Southern Alps glaciers, taking a breather on a Canterbury to West Coast transit flight.

Pūkeko lack webbed feet but are adequate swimmers and have a good balance in the water, on land or in trees.

While they look very attractive in the wild, they are, in fact, quite aggressive and will attack, eating eggs and killing chicks of other species in particular.

The culling of pūkeko on Great Barrier Island by the Department of Conservation has been a significant part of the programme to restore the population of little brown teal.

HUNTING PŪKEKO

Pūkeko have been harvested game birds in New Zealand for generations.

The blue body feathers are prime fly-tying material for classic night lures such as Craig's Night-Time, Taihape Tickler, and Scotch Poacher.

Many kākahu (cloak) weavers are keen to access pūkeko feathers, so why not ask your local marae or DOC office if they would like some clean, dry feathers?

Pūkeko have excellent hearing and eyesight and can be very challenging to hunt once they wise up to hunting.

However, in dim light or high winds, they are much easier to approach.

Another exciting technique is to flush them from raupō swamps using a good dog.

WHERE TO FIND PŪKEKO

Pūkeko population numbers vary in different parts of the country, and there is a lower daily bag limit in some regions.

In other regions with higher rainfall and lower-lying areas, pūkeko numbers are higher; therefore, the bag limit is also higher in some areas.

In some of these regions, their numbers are having an adverse effect on agriculture.

In response to reports of damage to crops and horticulture, several Fish & Game regions have special seasons to reduce bird numbers at high-risk sites through a harvest outside of the main game season.

On the West Coast of the South Island, a significant increase in the total area of improved pasture throughout much of the region has led to pūkeko populations becoming more widely distributed. Large concentrations of up to 200 to 300 birds are now typical on properties where the habitat is exceptionally favourable.

Since 2000, Fish & Game has monitored pūkeko in this region using a combination of roadside transects and static counts.

In the region, annual fluctuations at monitoring sites are common due to a tendency for flocks to be quite mobile.

However, the long-term trend shows the overall West Coast population has averaged 3% growth per annum.

PREPARATION:

It will surprise many hunters to know pūkeko can be delicious.

The secret is not to overcook them, or the old story about cooking them with a rock to weigh them down in the pot, or cooking them with an old boot for four hours, throwing away the pūkeko and eating the rock or boot, will come true!

When cooked right and offered to the public to sample, the verdict has been 100% positive.

An easy method is to remove the breast meat, place it on a cutting board and with a sharp knife, cut horizontally along these breasts to make two schnitzels from each, more if they are large breasts.

Beat these somewhat with a meat bat to make the meat thickness even.

A simple recipe is to coat them in seasoned flour, pass them through an egg wash, then breadcrumbs.

This is a reliable and straightforward recipe, but just remember not to fry it too long.

Make a suitable sauce and lay the cooked schnitzels on it.

– John Dyer, Fish & Game New Zealand

PŪKEKO BURGER

Abundant and widespread, the native pūkeko flourishes in most parts of New Zealand. They are large birds and are sometimes called swamphens. Their meat is often underrated but is delicious and tender, and there's plenty to go around!

PATTY

300g **pūkeko breasts**, minced

¼ **white onion**, sliced

1 Tbsp **cooking oil**

Pinch of **paprika**

1 clove **garlic**, sliced

2 slices **beetroot**

Knob of **butter**

2 **rashers bacon**

3 pinches of **salt**

2 pinches of **pepper**

TO SERVE

2 **brioche buns**

2 Tbsp **mayonnaise**

½ handful of **mesclun salad**

1 Tbsp **Rich Red Tamarillo Chutney** (see page 31)

4 slices **cheddar**

Preheat the oven to 180°C.

Add the cooking oil to a hot frying pan and brown the onion, adding the smoked paprika and garlic. Next add 2 thin slices of beetroot and fry until cooked through. Into a separate hot frying pan, add the bacon with a knob of butter and fry until golden brown. Set aside.

Transfer the cooked onions and garlic into a large bowl and add the minced pūkeko, adding salt and pepper and mix well, using your hands to shape the mixture into two patties.

Into a hot pan, with a knob of butter, brown the patties for 3-4 minutes on both sides. Then place in the oven for 10 minutes to cook the patty through.

To stack each burger, halve a brioche bun, spreading a dollop of mayonnaise on the base. Place some salad, followed by the patty and a dollop of chutney. Top with cheese, beetroot and bacon to finish.

Close the burger with the other half of the bun and voilà!

The messier the better!

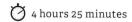

BIRD

1 **whole pūkeko**

1 **large oven bag**

Knob of **butter**

3 Tbsp **port**

1 sprig **thyme**

1 sprig **rosemary**

4 **sage leaves**

3 pinches of **salt**

3 pinches of **pepper**

MASH

4 **medium agria potatoes**, diced

25g **butter**

¼ cup **milk**

¼ cup **frozen peas**

4 pinches of **salt**

4 pinches of **pepper**

Grated cheese

FILLING

100g **butter**

2 **white onions**, sliced

6 cloves **garlic**, chopped

2 rashers **bacon**, chopped

1 tsp **Rub-A -Dub Duckie Rub**
(see page 37)

4 **carrots**, chopped

10 **yams**, chopped

1L **beef stock**

½ cup **port**

250g **'ready to eat' pitted prunes**

1 Tbsp **black pepper**

3 Tbsp **Worcestershire sauce**

PASTRY

Butter for greasing

Pre-made short savoury pastry

PŪKEKO POTATO-TOP PIE

This is a dish that's well worth the wait. While it takes a bit of time to prep, once you're done and it's in the oven you're good to go. And the result is so good you'll be glad you put in the effort!

Preheat the oven to 160°C.

Into an oven bag add the bird along with the butter, port, thyme, rosemary, sage leaves, salt and pepper. Tie the bag and make a small incision in the bag to let the steam out. Place in the oven for 3 hours. Once cooked allow to cool for 15-20 minutes. Turn the oven up to 180°C. Empty the bird and the juices into a bowl. Shred the meat off the bones (being careful to avoid small bones). Set aside.

For the mash, in a saucepan add the potatoes to boiling water and cook for 15-20 minutes or until soft. Drain and place back into the same saucepan. Add the butter and milk and start mashing the potato until smooth. Stir in the peas and season with salt and pepper. Set aside.

In a large hot pan, use the butter to brown the onions, garlic and bacon. Turning the heat down slightly, add your rub, carrots, yams and the beef stock and let simmer for 35 minutes, stirring occasionally. Then add the shredded bird meat and juices, port, prunes, black pepper and Worcestershire sauce. Simmer for a further 20 minutes. Set aside to cool.

Pre-grease a large pie dish and line the dish with pastry. Pour the cooled filling mixture into the dish and top with the potato and pea mash, spreading it evenly with your fingers and patting down until flat. Sprinkle grated cheese on top.

Place into the 180°C oven for 25 minutes. Then turn down to 120°C and cook for a further 15 minutes or until golden brown.

Take out of the oven and dig in.

PŪKEKO CORNISH PASTIES

Like pies, a pastie is a lunchtime favourite of old-school New Zealand. Cornish pasties are tasty pockets of meat and veg, filling and versatile and great for pūkeko meat. These are a perfect and easy, healthy, hearty snack or lunch to take on a hunt or to the maimai – and the kids will love them too!

BIRD

300g **minced pūkeko breast**

FILLING

35g **butter**

½ **white onion**, diced into 0.5cm pieces

1 **carrot**, diced into 0.5cm pieces

½ **medium potato**, diced into 0.5 cm pieces

3 **sage leaves**, chopped

1 Tbsp **Worcestershire sauce**

½ tsp **wholegrain mustard**

6 pinches of **salt**

2 pinches of **black pepper**

2 Tbsp **Rich Red Tamarillo Chutney** (see page 31)

PASTRY

3 sheets **pre-made savoury short pastry** (about A4 size)

1 **egg yolk**

Preheat oven to 180°C.

In a deep, hot frying pan, add the butter and brown the onion, carrot and potato.

While they sauté, add your sage leaves, Worcestershire sauce, mustard, salt and pepper. Add the minced pūkeko meat and stir it all together until the meat is cooked.

Stir in the chutney, ensuring all the ingredients are well mixed.

Set aside to cool.

Cut the pastry into 6 circles of roughly 6 inches or 15cm across (I use a small plate to stencil around). Add 3 Tbsp of filling mixture to the centre of each pastry sleeve. Fold the pastry over the filling mixture to form a semi-circle and press on the edges to seal the pastry together, then crimp to ensure the seal won't give way. Repeat along the pastry until the filling is sealed. Brush the pasty with egg yolk.

Use the fork prongs to scrape the egg yolk lightly over the pastry to create a pattern.

Place in the oven for 25 minutes or until golden brown.

Serve with a tomato relish or chutney.

TIP: If you don't have a pastry brush, a paper towel works just as well.

The black swan is an Australian bird that was introduced to New Zealand by the early acclimatisation societies. They liberated a total of 153 birds on 24 different occasions across Aotearoa between 1861 and 1871. Black swans quickly spread into all the available habitats, and large flocks were soon on the game bird licence.

However, from the 1970s on, farm silt run-off killed the water plants that swans depended on. Starving birds began eating grass and competing with farmers, leading to culls in which many thousands of the birds were killed until their numbers adapted to their impoverished circumstances.

Swan numbers remain strong in other areas where water plants persist, so most Fish & Game regions can allow limited swan hunting opportunities.

The issue of lake pollution, and therefore the swans' future, is one in which Fish & Game New Zealand takes a particular interest.

Swans often fly off lakes in the evening, allowing well-positioned hunters to intercept them under their flight lines.

Swans are also often shot as incidental birds while waiting for ducks. They certainly make an impressive splash when brought down from up high.

PREPARATION:

At one time, swans were a special occasion dish in the UK served only to royalty who had exclusive rights to them.

Most Kiwi hunters these days combine them with other game meats to create sausages and salamis.

Black swans are delicious to eat if properly prepared. Like all game, the meat is healthy and lean, but this means you need to be careful not to dry it out, for instance, by roasting it longer than necessary.

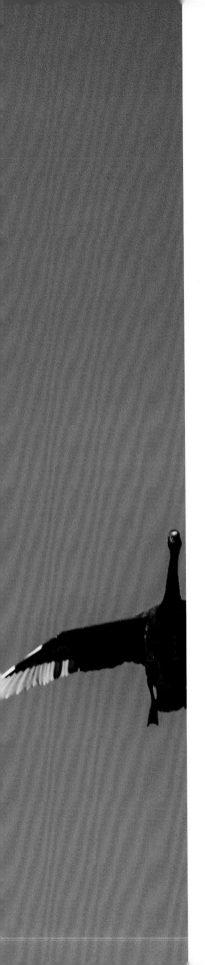

Swans are often quite gamey, especially older birds, identified by having jet-black plumage rather than dusky grey. This gaminess can be countered in several ways; for instance, if you use a slow cooker, use red wine to cover the chopped pieces instead of water. Start by searing the meat, fry some onions with it, add some crushed garlic, and lastly, the red wine and any root vegetables in the cupboard, such as chopped carrots, parsnips, celery, etc. It will smell delicious when ready.

An alternative is to soak swan (or any game) meat overnight before cooking in buttermilk, which you'll find in supermarkets in cartons. One marinade suggestion is to use red wine, olive oil, lemon juice and crushed garlic – marinate in the fridge overnight in a non-metal container with cling film to cover.

Many hunters schnitzel the breast meat. Cut it in 6-10mm thick slices, put these in a plastic bag (this will stop splatter), then beat with a plain-faced meat mallet to flatten the meat so it cooks evenly or use the textured side to tenderize. If you haven't got a meat bat, a champagne-style bottle is thick enough to safely use for the same purpose, or even a rolling pin.

Then dip in the usual flour, egg-wash and seasoned breadcrumbs. Or you can replace the breadcrumbs by whizzing up your favourite sesame crackers into a fine crumb. Or, instead of frying, some chefs then put these tenderised and coated meat strips into a baking dish and cover them with foil. Bake at 160°C for 40-50 minutes.

You can also skin the thighs and legs and confit these by cooking them slowly in duck fat which comes in jars. Or make a stew with onion and various root veggies and cook a good 2-3 hours, depending on how old the bird is.

– John Dyer, Fish & Game New Zealand

BLACK SWAN MEATLOAF WRAPPED IN BACON

Not your average meatloaf – this black swan version is full of flavour and goodness. Hearty, healthy, and tasty, it's a perfect snack on the go. Wrap it in a clean damp tea towel or add to a sandwich, everyone will be wanting to swap their lunch!

1kg **swan breast** (approx. 2 breasts), minced

100g **butter**

1½ **white onions**, diced

5 cloves **garlic**, chopped

20 **black grapes**

¼ tsp **dried thyme**

1 Tbsp **fresh rosemary**, chopped

1 **bay leaf**

1 Tbsp **fresh sage**, chopped

¼ tsp **smoked paprika**

¼ tsp **cinnamon**

4 pinches of **salt**

4 pinches of **pepper**

1 Tbsp **tomato paste**

½ cup **dried cranberries**

1½ cups **panko breadcrumbs**

1 whole **egg**

Butter for greasing

8 rashers **streaky bacon**

Cheese of your choice, sliced

Preheat oven to 180°C.

In a large, hot frying pan, melt the butter and cook the onions, garlic, grapes, herbs, spices, salt and pepper until golden brown. Stir in tomato paste and cook for a further 5 minutes. Remove from the heat and transfer the mixture into a large bowl. Remove the bay leaf, add the swan mince, cranberries, breadcrumbs and egg. Using your hands, combine all the ingredients.

Grease two loaf tins with butter. Line both tins with the bacon strips along the bottom of the tin allowing plenty of overhang on both sides. Pour half the meatloaf mixture into the tins, pressing down with your fingers. Arrange the cheese slices on top. Add the remaining mince mixture covering the cheese and once again pressing down to compact the loaf. Fold in the overhanging bacon stripes to cover the top of the loaf. Place in the oven for 35-40 minutes.

Once the meatloaf is cooked, allow to cool for 15-20 minutes before removing it from the tin. Let rest for a few minutes and serve.

Voila, a meatloaf to remember!

TIP: To grease the tins I recommend using butter instead of oil because it gives the dish a lovely buttery salty taste.

BLACK SWAN CURRIED SCHNITZEL BURGER

Introducing the black swan burger! Similar in taste and colour to venison, you may be pleasantly surprised by the flavour punch delivered by the black swan.

BIRD

1 **black swan breast**

2 **eggs**

½ cup **Curry In A Hurry Crumbed Rub** (see page 37)

25g **butter**

TO SERVE

4 **brioche buns**

Handful of **rocket salad**

Handful of **Pickled Cucumber** (see page 35), optional

2 **spring onion stalks**, chopped

½ handful of **mint leaves**

Spiced Mint Yoghurt Sauce (see page 32)

Preheat the oven to 170°C.

Remove the skin and sinew from the breast. Fillet the breast in half, creating 2 thinner breast fillets.

Using a mallet or rolling pin, tenderise the meat.

In a large bowl, whisk two eggs and submerge the fillets in the beaten eggs. Roll the egg-coated breasts in the crumbed rub. Cover the whole fillets with rub.

In a large, hot oven-proof pan, fry-off the 2 fillet schnitzels in butter until golden brown on both sides and place the schnitzels in the oven for 10 minutes.

To build the burger, start with the brioche bun base, layering the mint yoghurt sauce first, then rocket, followed by the schnitzel, pickled cucumber, spring onions and mint. Close with the brioche bun top to finish.

Burger up!

10 minutes   45 minutes   Serves 2

PAN-FRIED BLACK SWAN WITH BLACKBERRY SAUCE

Dark game meats go oh-so well with blackberries! And while in Aussie these birds aren't on the hunting list, in New Zealand we've got an abundance of them. And boy… do they taste delicious!

SAUCE

1 cup **frozen blackberries**

1 Tbsp **soft brown sugar**

3 Tbsp **water**

2 Tbsp **fig balsamic vinegar**

2 Tbsp **red wine**

BIRD

1 **swan breast**

30g **butter**

2 Tbsp **fresh thyme**, chopped

Pinch of **salt**

3 pinches of **black pepper**

Preheat the oven to 170°C.

Heat a saucepan and add the blackberries, sugar, water and balsamic, stirring occasionally. Simmer for about 3 minutes and then add the red wine. Continue to simmer for a further 10-15 minutes or until thickened. Set aside.

While the blackberries are thickening, in a hot, oven-proof frying pan melt the butter and add thyme, salt and pepper. Pan-sear the breast for 4-6 minutes, turn over and cook the other side for another 4-6 minutes.

Transfer the pan into the oven to cook the breast for a further 10 minutes.

Let the breast rest for 10 minutes before serving with the blackberry sauce.

TIP: This recipe cooks the meat to medium-rare but cooking times may vary depending on the thickness and size of the breast. Cook to your liking.

SAUCE

4 Tbsp **light olive oil**

1 **red onion**, sliced

4 cloves **garlic**, sliced

175g **vine sweet peppers**, sliced

¾ tsp **smoked paprika**

½ tsp **chipotle**

¼ tsp **cumin**

¼ tsp **pepper**

1 tsp **dried oregano**

½ tsp **dried thyme**

¼ tsp **ground coriander seeds**

¼ tsp **cinnamon**

1 **bay leaf**

3 x 400g **tinned crushed tomatoes**

1 Tbsp **tomato paste**

1 **chicken stock cube**

¼ tsp **salt**

salt & **black pepper**

BIRD

3 Tbsp **olive oil**

1 **red onion**, peeled and sliced

2 cloves **garlic**, finely chopped or minced

1 **whole red chilli**, deseeded and chopped

¼ tsp **ground coriander seeds**

¼ tsp **ginger**

¼ tsp **lemon pepper**

¼ tsp **smoked paprika**

2 Tbsp **raisins** (optional)

5 pinches of **salt**

5 pinches of **coarse black pepper**

1kg **swan breast**, minced

2 Tbsp **plain flour**

1 **egg**

Handful of **fresh parsley**, finely chopped

SPANISH BLACK SWAN MEATBALLS IN A SPICY TOMATO SAUCE

Minced black swan meat is a super healthy alternative to beef and can be frozen in freezer bags for future meals.

For the sauce: In a large, hot saucepan, use the olive oil to sauté the red onion, garlic cloves and sweet peppers. Add the spices and bay leaf, and cook for about 3 minutes or until golden brown. Lowering the heat, add the tinned tomatoes, tomato paste, crumbled chicken stock cube and salt. Stir ingredients together and simmer for up to 2 hours.

For the bird: As the sauce is simmering away, in a hot frying pan, brown the red onion, garlic and chilli with 1 Tbsp of olive oil until golden brown. Add the coriander, ginger, lemon pepper and smoked paprika and stir. Turn the heat off and stir in the raisins. Season with salt and black pepper and stir.

Place the minced meat into a large bowl with the fried onions, garlic, chilli and spice mix. Add the flour, egg and parsley. Mix well to bind the ingredients together. Grab a portion of minced meat mixture and, using your hands, roll into a ball. Repeat until the mixture is used up.

Brown the meatballs using 2 Tbsp of olive oil in a hot frying pan, making sure all sides of the balls are brown. Place the meatballs into the simmering sauce and cook for a further 30 minutes. Avoid over-stirring at this point as this could break apart the balls.

Serve this gorgeous meal sprinkled with freshly chopped parsley and a helping of crusty bread to mop up the sauce. Heaven!

TIP: The longer you cook the sauce the richer it will taste. I recommend using a non-stick saucepan.

UPLAND GAME

QUAIL • PHEASANT

QUAIL

Quail hunting is an exciting and demanding form of game bird hunting as they are small, fast-flying birds, which means quick and accurate shooting is required.

Californian quail were introduced to Auckland and Nelson in the 1860s, and other parts of New Zealand soon followed.

Today quail are the most common upland game bird in both the North and South Islands.

New Zealand has three species of quail: California, brown and bobwhite.

California quail are spread throughout New Zealand, while brown are very localised, and only very occasionally are bobwhite quail encountered in the North Island.

They prefer semi-arid conditions such as coastal dune areas, exotic forests, scrubby shingle river beds, and hill country.

Quail are likely to roost in briar, broom, boxthorn, matagouri, manuka or gorse.

You can also find them in scrubby areas on the edge of orchards and similar vegetation boundaries.

Californian quail are a challenge to hunt; they are noisy, 'talkative' birds making it easy to identify where a group or 'covey' may be resting, but their rapid speed and small size make shooting them challenging.

An undisturbed covey will sit tightly on the ground or in bushes.

When they are flushed by the hunter or by the hunter's dog, the birds explode quickly into the air, sometimes all at once, but other times in separate bursts, so stay alert!

When a covey is flushed, it is essential that the hunter picks out individual birds to shoot and gives them plenty of lead.

Quail do not fly long distances and will quickly return to the ground where they re-group and sit tight, so exciting hunting can occur in a reasonably small area.

The birds will call to each other to regroup, and a hunter with a quail-call can sometimes take advantage of this if they are patient.

The ideal weather conditions for quail hunting differ from that of duck hunting; bright, warm, sunny days are the most productive as in these conditions, the birds will be calling and moving about.

Gun dogs are an essential asset when quail hunting as the birds are small and can be difficult to flush and even harder to find when shot.

Retrievers such as labradors and spaniels will flush coveys and retrieve shot game.

Pointing dogs love the smell of quail and are useful for finding them afterwards.

EQUIPMENT:

Open choke shotguns are recommended in conjunction with number 7 or 8 shot.

Due to the rugged terrain and warmer weather, quail hunting requires different clothing than waterfowl hunting – lightweight boots and clothing.

Because quail hunters often hunt in a group staggered across a line, hunters often use a brightly coloured hunting vest or hat as a safety item.

PREPARATION:

Like all game meat, quail will taste a lot better if the shot birds have been quickly allowed to cool and kept that way until they are processed for the freezer.

So don't pile up shot quail or leave them in a hot 4WD; instead, hang them in the shade and allow the air to circulate around them.

You can pluck quail dry; just go carefully so as not to tear the delicate skin.

As with pheasants, turkeys, peafowl, chickens and partridge, but not waterfowl, quail will be much easier to pluck if they have been held by the legs and dunked up and down for 10 seconds or so in hot water around 60-70 degrees Celsius.

The feathers then almost rub off when you run your thumb along them, and plucking time is much reduced.

The skin is also less likely to tear; you can achieve the same effect by leaving upland game birds in the fridge overnight.

This allows the muscles holding back the feathers to relax before you pluck them.

The quail crop needs to be removed, and it may well contain weed seeds such as gorse, a favourite pheasant/quail cover.

Brown quail are relatively small birds, so it is pretty surprising how much meat is on them, resembling a rather tasty chicken.

This applies even more so for the bigger Californian quail.

– John Dyer, Fish & Game New Zealand

THE STAR OF NEW ZEALAND'S UPLAND GAME SPECIES

Chi-cago Chi-cago: the call of the Californian quail rings out from Angelo's quail caller as we silently move up the hillside looking for these elusive game birds.

We've arrived before dawn in the Upper Hakataramea Valley to hunt quail on Ken and Fiona Bowmar's high-country station.

Winter is harsh in the Hakataramea; from Cattle Creek, we are above the snow line, and the gravel road is set solid with a layer of ice.

Snow is all around in varying depths and means we can't drive up over the hill to the back of Ken & Fiona's farm; it's just too dangerous.

We have to hunt the front country where we can drive on the flat and walk up the hills.

We've joined Hamish Stevens and his dog Teal and Rhys Adams for the hunt today; after some quick local intel from Ken, it's gear on, and it's up the hill we go in search of these elusive cheeky birds.

It's not necessary to hunt quail in the snow and ice; they are widespread and plentiful from subalpine to coastal areas throughout the country.

We've come here today mainly because the Hakataramea is just a stunningly beautiful place to be.

Hidden away on the north side of the Waitaki River opposite Kurow, most Kiwis don't even know where it is – and the locals are pretty happy about that!

NZHistory online tells me the Hakataramea is named after a dance that took place near the mouth of the river, in which the performers wore bags made from the skin of the whekau (a native owl that is now extinct) filled with sweet-scented gum from the flower stalks of the taramea.

Its most famous son, Richie McCaw, without doubt the greatest All Black of all time, was born and raised here.

I have no doubt the extremes of the environment in the Hakataramea Valley shaped his character and created the resilience that rugby fans worldwide are in awe of.

Today the team will need a small dose of that resilience as the quail show just how hard they are to hunt.

As they have the ability to fly, land, and run away to pop up somewhere totally unexpected, all senses are needed to be on alert all of the time.

With a flash of feathers, the first covey of quail are spooked, and all eyes are on the birds to see where they land.

A plan is quickly hatched, and the team spread out, ready as Hamish and Teal close in to see what they can flush out.

Teal dives into the snow headfirst, a bunch of birds break cover and head straight at Rhys, and in a flash, they are gone.

While Rhys is a seasoned hunter, this is his first-ever quail hunt, and he's just learnt the hard way how quick these cunning birds are.

A great thing about quail is they don't go too far, and everyone repositions to have another go at them.

To get there means checking some prime quail habitat on the way, an occasional quail is spooked, and this time we all learn the lesson of just how fast these birds are.

We head downhill through the snow and ice to check out the first covey that got past us, the realisation dawning on us that quail hunting is not easy, it isn't a turkey shoot, and that these cunning little birds have suitably humbled our estimations of our abilities.

Our hunters close in on their quarry, and Teal shows us all how valuable a good dog is to hunt success.

Once again, in a quick flash, birds are airborne, but this time the hunt is successful as Angelo and Hamish connect with their shots.

Teal once again shows how vital a good dog is by recovering the birds in seconds.

Success can be a huge motivator, and today's hunt isn't just a hunt; there's a bit of pressure to source birds for the cookbook images.

So, it's with a partial sense of relief that we head to our second site with some birds in hand, but a few more are needed for the plate.

Hamish and Rhys take to the riverbed as we stay high as a cut off for any bird they disturb.

It doesn't take long, and a covey of about 40 birds are airborne, closely followed by six fallow deer, but our focus is on the quail.

Following them up the hillside, we close in on the quail.

Standing further back, I witness just how elusive these birds can be as two quail glide into the trees in front of me; they then scamper across the ground for about 30 metres before disappearing into the bush.

As I am armed only with a camera, they were initially safe from me; however, I call in the team, and we close in on these birds.

A few minutes later, Teal is back at work, and not long after, more birds are flushed, and now with the team's eyes in, more birds are downed.

With birds in hand, we finish up for the day and head back to the vehicles to clean up our birds.

As the quail feathers blow away across the snow, we all reflect on a good day hunting and the star of the show – Teal – gets a good belly rub from everyone.

– Richard Cosgrove, Fish & Game New Zealand

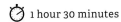

YORKSHIRE PUDDING

4 **whole eggs**

200ml **milk**

200g **plain flour**, sieved

Salt

Cooking oil spray

Rice bran oil

BIRD

4 **whole quail**

4 rashers **streaky bacon**

1 Tbsp **light olive oil**

1 **white onion**, quartered

3 **gourmet carrots**, halved

4 cloves **garlic**

4 large **sage leaves**

40g **butter**, roughly chopped

Up Your Game Pepper Steak Seasoning (see page 39)

MASH

1kg **kūmara**, peeled and diced

3 cups **water** for boiling

Pinch of **salt**

30g **butter**

¼ cup **cream**

1 Tbsp **parmesan cheese**, grated

salt & **pepper**

GRAVY

Upland Gravy Baby
(see page 34)

TIP: The key to good Yorkshire puddings is to pour the batter onto hot oil and don't open the oven door while they cook!

ROAST QUAIL NESTS

Now this is decadence! A whole quail to yourself nestled in a Yorkshire pudding! Royalty, here I come. Makes you really look forward to Sunday!

Preheat the oven to 200°C.

Whisk the eggs into a large bowl, add the milk and whisk together. Then add the flour, whisking to form a smooth batter. Finish by adding a couple pinches of salt. Spray cooking oil into four pie tins. Add a splash of rice bran oil to coat the bottom of the tins. Place in the oven for 15 minutes. Once the oil is very hot, carefully pour your batter just over half full into the tins. Place back into the oven to cook for 20-25 minutes. It's important to dedicate the whole oven for your Yorkshire puddings to get the best result. Once cooked, set aside.

Turn the oven down to 170°C.

Tie together the legs on each individual bird with butcher's string. Halve your streaky bacon into thinner rashers and wrap each bird with two thin rashers. Next brush the birds with light olive oil and place in an oven dish. Add the quartered onion and carrots to the dish. Take one garlic clove per bird and wrap the sage leaf around it, placing the sage wrapped garlic clove on top of each bird. Scatter the butter pieces over the dish and sprinkle with the pepper steak seasoning. Place in the oven for 35 minutes.

In a hot saucepan, add the kūmara, cover with water and bring to the boil. Turn the heat down to a simmer and cook for 15 minutes or until soft. Drain and run cold water over the kūmara.

Mash the kūmara in the saucepan, adding butter, cream, and a sprinkling of parmesan to create a smooth, creamy consistency. Season with salt and pepper. Don't be afraid to add more salt to your liking.

Assemble your nests by placing the mash inside the Yorkshire puddings with the quail, carrots and onions popped on top and, of course, a generous helping of gravy!

CHARCOAL-GRILLED QUAIL WITH BABY BEETS & APPLES

Cut through the rich smoky flavour of deliciously chargrilled quail with heady and tart apples and beets. Full of rich and healthy goodness, this is a dish to be enjoyed slowly with great company. Using brine softens the muscle fibres, helping to tenderise the meat.

BRINE

2 Tbsp **salt**

1 Tbsp **sugar**

1L **water**

SIDE

100g **melted butter**

12 **small apples**

250g **baby beetroot**, halved

12 whole cloves **garlic**

60ml **pomegranate molasses**

4 pinches of **Up Your Game Pepper Steak Seasoning** (see page 39)

4 pinches of **flaky salt**

BIRD

7 **quail**, halved

¼ cup **olive oil**

5 pinches of **flaky salt**

½ tsp **lemon pepper**

½ tsp **dried thyme**

SAUCE

Apricot & Bourbon BBQ Sauce (see page 32)

To make the brine, dissolve the salt and sugar in the water. Soak the birds in brine overnight.

Preheat the oven to 170°C.

In a large bowl, drizzle the melted butter over the apples and beetroot, tossing through until covered. Transfer into an oven-proof dish, adding the garlic and drizzling over the pomegranate molasses. Season with pepper steak seasoning and salt. Place in the oven for 45 minutes or until softened.

To prepare the birds, halve each quail down the spine and pat dry with paper towels. In a large bowl, coat the quail in olive oil and season with salt, lemon pepper and thyme. Place the birds skin-side down on the BBQ, turning over every so often to ensure even cooking, for 10-15 minutes or until the flesh appears white and the juices run clear.

Drizzle the BBQ sauce over the charcoal-grilled birds, beets and roast apples.

Enjoy!

HERB-BUTTERED ROAST QUAIL WITH LEMON THYME SAUCE

This dish is a true celebration that'll have your dinner guests coming back 'thyme' after 'thyme'. I find that quail dishes really bring out the inner chef in us all and there's nothing better than sharing these very special meals with friends.

BIRD

3 **whole quail**

1 Tbsp **extra virgin olive oil**

4 whole heads **garlic**, skin on

10 **shallots**, halved

420g **artichoke hearts in brine**

2 **lemons**, quartered

8 sprigs **thyme**

1 Tbsp **fresh rosemary**, chopped

Salt & **pepper**

3 Tbsp **Herb Butter** (see page 39)

7 dried **'ready to eat' figs**

4 pinches of **salt**

4 pinches of **pepper**

LEMON THYME SAUCE

3 roasted cloves **garlic**

Juice of ¾ **roasted lemon**

2 Tbsp **roasting juices**

3 **roasted thyme sprigs**, destalked

1 cup **chicken stock**

½ cup **cream**

¼ cup **white wine**

2 pinches of **black pepper**

¾ tsp **arrowroot**

Preheat the oven to 180°C.

In a large hot pan, brown the garlic, shallots, artichokes and lemons in the olive oil. Throw into a roasting dish with the thyme and rosemary and season generously with salt and pepper.

Tie the legs of the quail with butcher's string. In a pan on a medium heat, lightly brown the quail in 1 Tbsp of herb butter until golden brown. Add the birds to the roasting dish. Scatter the remaining 2 Tbsp of herb butter and the figs into the roasting dish. Roast in the oven for 30 minutes.

To make the sauce, take 3 cloves of the roasted garlic and squash with a fork to remove the skins. Into a saucepan add the garlic with a squeeze of the roasted lemon juice, roasting juices from the quail and 3 roasted thyme sprigs. Pour the chicken stock into the pan with the cream and white wine, and simmer. Add the pepper and the arrowroot to thicken the sauce, stirring continually for roughly 2 minutes or until the desired consistency is achieved.

Voilà! Your creamy, light, lemon and thyme sauce is ready to pour over this beautifully simple quail dish.

TIP: For a more substantial meal, add mashed or roast potatoes.

PHEASANT

Pheasants are one of New Zealand's most sought-after game birds.

Their bright plumage and superb eating qualities make them popular with all game bird hunters.

The first English (blackneck) pheasants arrived in Wellington in 1842, and further liberations throughout the country resulted in the bird being abundant in both islands by 1870. The Chinese ringneck was introduced by Thomas Henderson in 1851 in the Auckland suburb that now bears his name. The current wild bird is a mixture.

The pheasant population then plunged into a remarkable decline, from which it has never recovered, due to eating poisoned grain used for rabbit eradication followed by the release of ferrets, stoats and weasels to quell the rabbit plague. Introduced small birds also played a significant role in competing for the same food.

For many years acclimatisation societies reared and released thousands of pheasants but eventually came to rely on the natural production by birds already well established in the wild. In part, the almost universal protection of wild hen pheasants ensured that these wild populations have always filled out the available habitat, as one cock pheasant can service many hens in the breeding season and maintain the huntable population.

The pheasant used to be called a North Island species with its stronghold in the warmer northern climes, mainly where plenty of natural cover remains. However, pheasants are now widespread in the South Island, with all regions offering a pheasant hunting season.

They are found in coastal dune country, exotic forestry, lupin, broom, box-thorn, and briar patches. Also, look for patches of inkweed, rough covered gullies and natural cover around harvested crops such as maize. Pheasants also feed on a wide range of berries, seeds, and other vegetation and also eat crickets and grasshoppers.

Pheasants have no down and dislike damp conditions. On cooler days, ignore areas in shadow and look for edges of cover still receiving the sun's rays. If it's more pleasant for you to be there, chances are the pheasant is thinking the same.

HUNTING PHEASANT:

In the North Island, pheasant hunting season generally begins on the first weekend of May and typically lasts until late August. In the South Island, Nelson Marlborough and North Canterbury have a wild pheasant season for three weekends only; the season runs for multiple weeks in the other South Island regions.

As regulations vary between each Fish & Game region, it is essential to check your local game bird hunting regulations.

Often exotic forestry blocks are available for pheasant hunting. Access permits are required and usually booked through the local Fish and Game Council. Your regulation booklet supplied with your licence will usually have this season length and access information in it. Many pheasants are shot on private land and a polite request to hunt some likely land is often the start of a great hunt. Please respect any conditions the landowner has, such as making sure the gates are always left open or shut, the way you found them.

HUNTING TIPS:

Pheasants have excellent hearing and eyesight. They're also very sensitive to vibration, so don't slam the car door and don't jump off that fence you're crossing.

Successful hunting requires elements of silence and surprise. Experienced advice is to not yell at your dog; use a whistle.

If you stand on a hill and listen to a pheasant hunter yelling at his dog, you can watch the pheasants escaping ahead of him.

When pheasants are flushed, they often glide for quite a distance before landing and running off at high speed.

Don't expect them to be near where they land, but it is an excellent place to start your dog.

Often pheasants will sit tight in dense vegetation. One trick is to stop frequently, which can unnerve a hiding bird in thinking that you've seen it and send it into flight. Be ready for him! If it is a young bird, experienced hunters let it escape to grow bigger.

You can also team up with other hunters to walk in a line through crops and flush pheasants ahead.

The best pheasant hunting occurs on bright days. Sunny spells have the birds moving about from daybreak to mid-morning and again from mid-afternoon to dusk.

If you flush a bird one day but don't give it too big a fright, there's a good chance you'll find it in much the same place, the same time the next day.

Try and outthink which way it might break cover and which nearest cover it might fly to and be there to intercept it.

GUN DOGS:

A good dog is almost essential as pheasants can be difficult to flush from cover.

Shot birds can also be challenging to find.

Breeds like labradors, pointers, and spaniels are very useful as they find, flush, and retrieve these birds. Be sure to keep your dog tied up when you're getting set up, or it might be flushing the birds while you're still getting ready.

EQUIPMENT:

Open choke shotguns offer hunters a good chance of bagging a pheasant.

Due to the typical terrain and weather, pheasant hunting requires different clothing than waterfowl hunting – lightweight boots and clothing.

Because pheasant hunters often hunt in a group through scrubby terrain, many hunters use brightly coloured hunting vests or hats as safety items.

Vests also have plenty of room for ammunition and retrieved birds.

More information: Your local Fish and Game Council is a good place to start your hunt, with access permits and helpful advice.

PREPARATION:

Plucking pheasants is simple enough. Pinch off a small number of feathers and pull against the grain. Stop when they are all gone! There's a great description in Angelo's Tips & Tricks on plucking and cleaning your game bird.

Once clean, remove the wings and head with a sharp pair of garden secateurs.

To remove leg sinews, take a sharp knife and cut around the knee joint to remove the skin only and just expose the pink beneath. Now double each leg over a 150mm long nail driven into a wall somewhere and pull down hard. All the sinews should come out with each leg. If you roast the bird and leave these sinews in, they'll dry out like bony toothpicks.

To eviscerate the bird, make a small cut in the throat area and another from the vent along the belly but not so deep as to cut entrails. Reach in and pull these out, including the heart, liver, lungs and windpipe. Remove the crop and see what it had been feeding on; it might be helpful to know next time. If you run an old hosepipe, water on, up and down the backbone, you'll loosen any remaining material. Then poke the hose down the hole in the throat area to wash from above. Stand vertical and allow to dry, then double-bag (having squashed any air out of the bag), label with the species and date, then freeze. Be sure to air out the room you did this cleaning in and, if the rubbish day is a week off, consider freezing the labelled entrails etc, until then. The severed wings can be added to dog training dummies to make practice more realistic. Trout fly tiers and makers of kākahu (cloaks) may also appreciate the offer of clean dry feathers.

Like all game birds, pheasants have lean and heart-healthy meat. This also means it is easy to dry them out if they are overcooked, whatever method is used. Some recipes call for the roasted bird's breast to be covered in fatty bacon. As the bacon cooks, its fat keeps the breast from drying out and afterwards, it makes a tasty side dish. You can also regularly baste the bird with the cooking liquid. Foil wrapped over the bird in an oven tray is another way to keep the meat from drying out. Roasting bags make life too easy. They keep the moisture and the ingredients in, while also stopping any splatter from getting onto the oven. Pheasants can also be poached (lightly simmered) in some recipes. Or try mincing the meat for sausages or a healthy meatloaf.

When is the bird done? Toward the end of the cooking period, cut any string trusses on the legs, open one leg/thigh slightly from the body, make a small incision in the skin joining the leg/body and look at the colour of the juices at the base of the joint. If they're red, keep cooking. If pink, that's good; you're close to done; give it another 10 minutes. If clear, you're there. If it's dry, stop at once!

Bon Appetit!

– John Dyer, Fish & Game New Zealand

GLAZED PHEASANT WITH FRAGRANT BASMATI RICE

Pheasants have been hunted for their stunning feathers and delicately flavoured meat since Roman times and remain a popular bird to bag the world over. It's got a nice, almost smoky flavour that makes it great to eat with a simple glaze and good hearty sauce.

BIRD

1 **whole pheasant**

1 tsp **sesame oil**

4 cloves **garlic**, sliced

2 thumbs of **ginger**, sliced

1 **red chilli**, sliced

6 Tbsp **sweet soy sauce**

4 pinches of **Chinese five spice**

Handful of **fresh coriander leaves**, chopped

1 pinch of **sesame seeds**

RICE

1½ cups **brown basmati rice**

4 cups **water** for boiling

¼ cup **orange blossom water** (optional)

TO SERVE

Fresh chopped coriander leaves

1 tsp **sesame seeds**

Dehydrated persimmon (optional)

Preheat the oven to 150°C.

Lightly brush the whole bird with sesame seed oil and place into the oven for 25 minutes. Remove from oven and set aside to rest. Turn the oven up to 160°C.

Once the bird has cooled, quarter the pheasant and place the sliced garlic, ginger and chilli on top of each quarter. Drizzle the sweet soy sauce over the bird and sprinkle a pinch of Chinese five spice over each quarter.

Roast in the oven for 40 minutes. Baste the bird every 10 minutes by carefully spooning the juices over the meat.

While the bird roasts, rinse your rice with cold water to wash away any starch. In a saucepan bring the water to the boil, then add the rice and orange blossom water. Reduce to a simmer and cook for 45 minutes, stirring occasionally.

Serve with fresh coriander and sesame seeds.

TIP: Baste the bird every 10 minutes to glaze the skin, allowing the bird to absorb all the flavours.

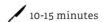 
PAN-FRIED PHEASANT WITH BABY WHITE BUTTERED TURNIPS

Combined with earthy, sweet turnips, this dish enhances the light, subtle flavour of the pheasant. Nice and simple and absolutely delicious!

SAUCE

Blueberry & Sage Sauce
(see page 30)

BIRD

1 **whole pheasant**

2 Tbsp **light olive oil**

1 Tbsp **Herb Butter**
(see page 39)

TURNIPS

2 Tbsp **butter**

250g **baby white turnips**, halved

2 pinches of **salt**

10 **sage leaves**

Quarter the whole pheasant and brown in a hot pan with olive oil and herb butter, covering with a lid.

Turn the heat to low and cook for a further 15-20 minutes until the bird is cooked through. Be mindful to occasionally turn the bird so it doesn't burn on one side. Remove from heat and set aside to rest.

While the pheasant is cooking, you can start on the turnips. In a large hot frying pan, add the butter and lightly brown the baby white turnips for 8-10 minutes, adding salt and the sage leaves. Turn the heat off and cover with a lid to soften the turnips for a further 5 minutes.

Plate up with the pheasant and Blueberry & Sage Sauce.

BIRD

1 **whole pheasant**, quartered

2 **whole sweet red peppers**

1 Tbsp **light olive oil**

3 cloves **garlic**, crushed

1 Tbsp **butter**

Handful of **fresh parsley**, chopped

2 Tbsp **chives**, chopped

10 sprigs **thyme**, chopped

10 **sage leaves**

Handful of **fresh rosemary**, chopped

1 **bay leaf**

Extra virgin olive oil

Rustic Ragu Sauce
(see page 31)

POLENTA

500ml **water**

1 **chicken stock cube**

½ cup **polenta**

50g **butter**

2 pinches of **cracked pepper**

½ cup **cream**

1 Tbsp **parmesan cheese**, grated

1 pinch of **nutmeg**

TIP: You can pre-make the polenta, set aside to cool and place in the fridge. Once the pheasant is ready, re-heat the polenta by placing it in a saucepan on medium heat stirring continually until heated throughout.

RUSTIC PHEASANT RAGU WITH SMOKED SWEET PEPPERS & POLENTA

This rustic Italian dish is one of my favourites in this cookbook. It makes you feel like you're really in a tiny rustic village in the heart of Italy. It brings a whole new meaning to comfort food!

Preheat a slow cooker to a medium setting, and prepare your smoker.

In a hot frying pan, heat the oil, garlic and butter until the butter is melted. Remove from the heat and brush the resulting garlic butter over the quartered bird and whole sweet peppers, before placing them in the smoker.

Allow the bird and peppers to hot smoke for 7 minutes. Let sit in the smoker for a further 3 minutes with no heat. Be careful not to over smoke the bird as it can taint the flavour of this dish. Set aside the sweet peppers.

Using the same hot frying pan with the residue of the garlic butter, pan-sear the pheasant for 5 minutes, adding all the herbs and turning over to evenly cook the joints, until the quarters are browned off.

Place the pheasant into the slow cooker with all the juices from the frying pan. In the same hot frying pan, pan-sear the smoked peppers on both sides with a drizzle of olive oil until charred and blistered. Cut in half and add to the slow cooker.

Add the Rustic Ragu Sauce to the slow cooker, place the lid on top and let simmer for 1 hour on medium. Turn the heat down to low and simmer for a further 2 hours.

For the polenta, in a large hot saucepan dissolve the chicken stock cube in boiling water. Bring to a simmer, add the polenta stirring regularly until thickened. Add butter, pepper and the cream, stirring in for 5-6 minutes. Remove from the heat and finish by adding the parmesan and nutmeg. The polenta should be smooth and creamy in consistency.

Dish up the pheasant ragu with your side of sweet peppers and polenta.

PHEASANT AU VIN

A personal favourite, this traditional French dish is absolutely brilliant with pheasant. Paired with tasty, easy sides, it's a fancy dish that's not hard to make fabulous! Perfect for a special dinner for two.

BIRD

1 **whole pheasant**, quartered

1 **large oven bag**

Up Your Game Pepper Steak Seasoning (see page 39)

Salt

2 Tbsp **extra virgin olive oil**

1 **onion**, quartered

3 cloves **garlic**, peeled

1 Tbsp **fresh thyme**, chopped

1 Tbsp **fresh flatleaf parsley**, chopped

¼ cup **white wine**

1 **bay leaf**

8 **small gourmet carrots**

2 pinches of **salt**

2 pinches of **pepper**

SAUCE

75g **butter**

¼ tsp **Up Your Game Pepper Steak Seasoning** (see page 39)

4 cloves **garlic**, sliced

160g **streaky bacon**, chopped

200g **white mushrooms**, sliced

¼ cup **white wine**

1 Tbsp **fresh thyme** or ¼ Tbsp dried

250g **thickened cream**

Preheat the oven to 160°C.

Season each pheasant quarter with pepper steak seasoning and salt.

Brown the quartered bird in a hot frying pan, adding the onion and garlic with the olive oil and herbs. Once golden brown on both sides, carefully transfer the bird and all ingredients (including the juices) from the frying pan into a large oven bag. Add the white wine, bay leaf, carrots, salt and pepper to the bag and tie. Pierce the bag near the tie to allow the steam to exit and place on a roasting dish to cook in the oven for 1 hour and 30 minutes.

Once cooked, remove the bird from the oven bag and set aside to rest.

For the sauce, in a large hot saucepan, melt the butter, add the pepper steak seasoning and brown the garlic. Sauté the bacon and mushrooms. Pour the contents from the oven bag into the pan, stirring in the white wine, thyme and thickened cream. Simmer for 5 minutes.

To serve, place the pheasant quarters into the sauce.

TIP: The dish is traditionally cooked with red wine but I prefer to cook it with white wine, giving it a cleaner taste.

BIRD

1 **whole pheasant**

1 **lemon**, cut in half

200g **cherry tomatoes**

3 cloves **garlic**, sliced

3 Tbsp **extra virgin olive oil**

2 pinches of **smoked paprika**

1 Tbsp **fresh rosemary**, chopped

1 Tbsp **fresh oregano**, chopped

3 pinches of **salt**

3 pinches of **coarse black pepper**

RISOTTO

25g **butter**

1 **sweetcorn cob**, leaves removed

1 **white onion**, finely diced

2 cloves **garlic**, finely diced

1 Tbsp **olive oil**

50g **butter**

300g **arborio rice**

1 cup **white wine**

2 cups **chicken stock**

½ cup **water**

½ cup **mascarpone cheese**

¼ cup **parmesan**, grated

½ tsp **Up Your Game Pepper Steak Seasoning** (see page 39)

½ cup **frozen peas**

TO SERVE

avocado oil

basil leaves (optional)

TIP: This is a great dish to create with any leftover pheasant from a roast.

CHARRED SWEETCORN & PEA RISOTTO WITH ROAST PHEASANT

What's the secret to a perfect risotto? Stir, stir, and stir again! Add liquid as required so it doesn't dry out and the rice stays succulent, yet firm. You want a slight crunch to it but soft enough to bite through.

Preheat the oven to 170°C.

Stuff half a lemon into the carcass of the bird and place into a large oven bag along with the cherry tomatoes, garlic, olive oil, paprika, rosemary, oregano, salt, pepper and a squeeze of lemon juice. Tie the bag (piercing a hole near the tie) and place in the oven for 1 hour 30 minutes. Set aside and let rest.

In a hot frying pan, melt butter and blister sweetcorn cob until all sides are dark golden brown. Remove from the heat and carefully slice the cob from top to bottom to release the kernels away from the cob. Set aside.

In a deep hot frying pan sauté your onion and garlic with olive oil and butter until transparent in colour. Add the rice with 1 cup of white wine and turn the heat down to a low simmer, stirring continuously. As the rice absorbs the liquid, gradually add a spoonful at a time of the chicken stock. Once the chicken stock has been used up, start adding water a spoonful at a time, stirring all the while. Finally add the mascarpone, parmesan and pepper steak seasoning. Stir in the peas and add the charred sweetcorn. This should take about 20 to 25 minutes.

Check if the rice is cooked; it should be soft enough to bite through with a slight crunch, and the dish should be smooth and creamy in consistency. If you like your rice soft, cook for longer, remembering to add more liquid.

Place your roast pheasant with all the components from the oven bag on top of the risotto.

Enjoy with a splash of avocado oil.

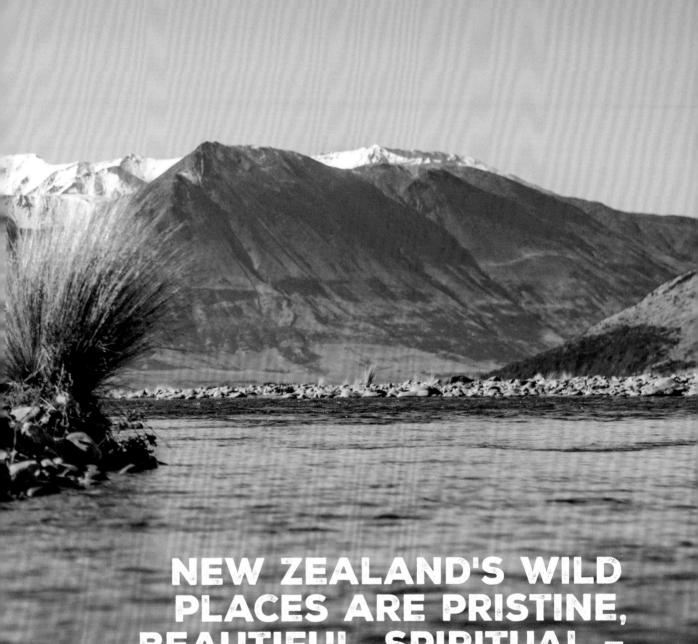

NEW ZEALAND'S WILD PLACES ARE PRISTINE, BEAUTIFUL, SPIRITUAL – LEAVE THEM AS YOU FOUND THEM, TAKING ONLY MEMORIES AND YOUR QUARRY WITH YOU

FISH

CHINOOK SALMON · RAINBOW TROUT · BROWN TROUT · PERCH

CHINOOK SALMON

Once you hook a salmon, it's not actually sure who is hooked – the fish or the human?

Many describe them as the 'silver bullet', the name inspired by the sight of these huge shiny silvery fish running the rapids of the big, braided rivers of the South Island as they head to their spawning grounds after a couple of years at sea.

Revered by anglers, they are the most addictive of sports fish. So compelling is the quest to harvest one that thousands of anglers will travel hundreds of kilometres and spend days lined shoulder to shoulder in a 'picket fence' just trying to catch one of these fish.

The annual Rakaia salmon fishing contest, for instance, brings over 700 anglers to one river for one weekend in the hope of catching salmon.

In the past, when word got out that there was a run on, such is the pull of these fish, anglers in their hundreds would drop everything and head for the rivers.

Chinook Salmon, also known as Quinnat Salmon, were successfully introduced to the South Island in 1901 in the Hakataramea River.

New Zealand was the only country of 14 requestors given salmon for release, which established a viable wild population.

They are the largest freshwater sports fish available to New Zealand anglers, and almost all are confined to several of the larger South Island rivers.

The Chinook salmon is also the largest of the Pacific salmon species: a large salmon may attain a weight of 15 kg or more; however, salmon of half this weight are more common.

Like all Pacific salmon species, they die after spawning.

The male and female of the species have different colouring, and a salmon caught in the surf, or the tidal area of a river, is predominantly silver, with the back being dark grey-green.

There are numerous small black spots on the back and the tail.

Once established in our rivers, salmon were also released into the chilly South Island alpine lakes and have thrived there, forming plentiful populations of landlocked lake salmon for anglers to harvest.

Lake salmon, which spend their entire life in freshwater, do not grow as big as anadromous (sea-run) salmon.

The spawning migration of Chinook salmon usually begins in December and will continue through the fishing season, with the peak of activity occurring about mid-March.

Anglers will commonly use longer and heavier spinning rods to cast the large silver spoons or wobblers that salmon strike at as they enter the river or journey to headwater spawning waters on their spawning run.

– Richard Cosgrove, Fish & Game New Zealand

ROAST WHOLE SIDE OF SALMON WITH A STRAWBERRY BALSAMIC GLAZE

I like to call this dish, 'the party pleaser'! Take it to a 'bring your own plate' summer gathering and you'll be sure to make the Christmas card list!

FISH

1 **whole salmon side**, deboned

1 Tbsp **soft brown sugar**

Fig balsamic vinegar

1 Tbsp **flaky sea salt**

GLAZE

1 Tbsp **soft brown sugar**

½ cup **white wine vinegar**

½ cup **water**

10 **strawberries**, quartered

2 Tbsp **fig balsamic vinegar**

Zest of 1 **lemon**

TO SERVE

Salads or **greens**

Place salmon into a large oven dish and rub the brown sugar over the fillet. Next drizzle the fig balsamic and sprinkle the flaky sea salt evenly over the flesh. Cover the dish and place in the fridge overnight.

The next day, in a bowl, dissolve the brown sugar in the white wine vinegar and water. Add the strawberries to this pickling solution and allow to soak for 1 hour 30 minutes.

Preheat the oven to 170°C. Place the salmon onto baking paper skin-side down. Drain the soaked strawberries and transfer them into a bowl and coat them with fig balsamic. Carefully place them over the salmon with a sprinkle of lemon zest. Place into the oven for 20 minutes.

Serve with an array of side salads.

GRILLED SALMON SALAD

Share and share alike. Summer is all about getting together and sharing a meal with loved ones. This Greek-style mezze platter is a perfect light meal everyone can enjoy.

FISH

2 **salmon fillets**, skin on

Salt & **pepper**

1 Tbsp **olive oil**

4 tsp **runny honey**

Juice of ½ **lemon**

4 fronds **dill**

ROAST GRAPES

Bunch of **grapes**

1 Tbsp **olive oil**

1 tsp **balsamic vinegar glaze**

Pinch of **salt**

Pinch of **pepper**

HALLOUMI

4 slices **halloumi**, 1cm thick

2 pinches of **coarse black pepper**

SALAD

4 handfuls of **rocket leaves**

½ **lemon**, juice

2 Tbsp **extra virgin olive oil**

1 Tbsp **pomegranate molasses**

Seeds of ½ **pomegranate**

Pinch of **salt**

Pinch of **pepper**

Preheat the oven on grill to 200°C.

Take your two salmon fillets and slice them down the centre from head to tail, dividing into 4 strips.

Skewer your salmon fillets by folding them back on themselves as you push them through the skewer. Season with salt and pepper.

Place the salmon skewers (skin-side facing down) over oiled baking paper and drizzle olive oil, honey, lemon juice and dill over each skewer. Place the salmon in the oven to grill for about 10 minutes, turning halfway through the cooking process. Take out of the oven to rest while you plate up the salad.

Roast the grapes in an oven dish with a drizzle of olive oil, balsamic glaze, salt and pepper, for 5 minutes or until blistered.

In a hot pan, brown the halloumi on both sides and sprinkle with coarse black pepper.

In a large bowl, add fresh rocket leaves, lemon juice, extra virgin olive oil, pomegranate molasses and pomegranate seeds. Toss through and season the salad with salt and pepper.

Plate up the salmon skewers, halloumi, grapes and salad on a platter for everyone to help themselves.

TIP: DO NOT salt the halloumi, it is naturally preserved in brine water so no extra salt is needed!

SALMON PASTRY PARCEL

Speaking of parties…this delicious pastry parcel loaded with flavour is a perfect way to feed the family over the holidays. Great for lunch or as a BYO plate for BBQ gatherings.

FISH

30g **butter**

3 handfuls of **baby spinach**

3 pinches of **salt**

3 pinches of **pepper**

¼ cup **mascarpone cheese**

8-10 sheets of **pre-made filo pastry**

Melted butter or **olive oil** for brushing

2 **salmon fillets**, (tail end) skin removed

12 **asparagus spears**, fresh or tinned

30g melted **garlic butter**

2 pinches of **salt**

2 pinches of **pepper**

SAUCE

Lemon & Dill Hollandaise Sauce (see page 33)

Preheat the oven to 170°C.

Into a hot pan add the butter and spinach with salt and pepper. Stir the mascarpone cheese into the spinach and butter until it's melted. Remove from heat and set aside.

Brush the pastry sheets with melted butter or olive oil, stack them and place one of the salmon fillets in the centre. Brush the fillet with melted garlic butter and sprinkle with salt and add pepper. Layer half the creamed spinach on top of the salmon fillet, add half of the asparagus spears. Repeat with another layer of salmon, creamy spinach and asparagus, season with salt and pepper to finish.

Carefully fold the filo pastry over the top of the salmon filling and roll the filling with the pastry wrapping around it to form a parcel. Pinch the ends of the pastry closed.

Place the salmon parcel into an oven dish lined with baking paper. Brush the pastry with garlic butter.

Place in the oven and cook for 35-40 minutes or until the pastry has turned golden brown. Turn off the oven and let it rest in the oven for a further 5 minutes.

To serve, cut the parcel in half and drizzle with the hollandaise sauce.

MIDDLE EASTERN CRUSTED SALMON

A beautifully simple way to enjoy the decadent flavour of fresh salmon. Perfect for sharing, this dish is a delectable centrepiece for any festive summer occasion.

FISH

1 **whole salmon side**, filleted, skin on

1 Tbsp **flaky salt**

2 Tbsp **pomegranate molasses**

40g **Middle Meats East Crumbed Rub** (see page 38, double the recipe)

Seeds of ½ **pomegranate**

1 tsp **olive oil**

1 tsp **black sesame seeds**

Pinch of **salt**

TO SERVE

Salads or **greens**

Preheat the oven to 160°C.

Take one whole side of filleted salmon. Sprinkle the flesh with flaky salt and drizzle with pomegranate molasses.

Spread the crumbed rub over the whole fish fillet, patting down in place using your fingers. Place in the oven for 25 minutes or until the crumb is golden brown.

To make a simple dressing: over a bowl, use your fingers to break apart the pomegranate, removing the white flesh and keeping the seeds. Add the olive oil, black sesame seeds and a pinch of salt. Mix together and place over the salmon.

Serve with salads.

TIP: For this dish and other dishes where you're not eating the skin, there is no need to descale the fish.

COUSCOUS

200g **Israeli couscous**

Water for boiling

1 Tbsp **olive oil**

4 cloves **garlic**, sliced

Pinch of **ground cumin**

Pinch of **fennel seeds**

Pinch of **black pepper**

15 **black grapes**, halved

1 tsp **pomegranate molasses**

2 handful of **parsley**, destalked and finely chopped

3 **spring onions**, finely chopped

200g **cherry tomatoes**, halved

½ **cucumber**, roughly chopped

Zest and **juice** of 1 **lemon**

1 Tbsp **fresh dill**, roughly chopped

2 Tbsp **fresh mint**, roughly chopped

1 Tbsp **black sesame seeds** (optional)

1 Tbsp **roasted pistachios** (optional)

Salt & **pepper**

FISH

1 **whole side salmon**, descaled and deboned

2 Tbsp **olive oil**

¼ tsp **whole fennel seeds**

¼ tsp **smoked paprika**

¼ tsp **cumin**

¼ tsp **coriander seed**

1 Tbsp **fresh dill,** chopped

2 pinches of **salt**

3 pinches of **ground black pepper**

3 pinches of **black sesame seeds**

10 **mint leaves**, chopped

BBQ SKEWERED SALMON WITH ISRAELI COUSCOUS TABBOULEH

Another summer salmon sizzler! There are so many incredible flavours in here, but they all just come together in a sensational flavour smash topped off brilliantly by the beautiful fresh barbequed salmon. Yum!

Put the couscous in a pan and add enough water to cover it by 5cm and boil for 10-15 minutes.

Drain and run cold water over the couscous to cool. Transfer into a bowl and mix the olive oil through the couscous to prevent it from clumping.

In a hot frying pan brown the garlic, cumin, fennel seeds and pepper in olive oil until golden brown. Transfer from the pan into a small bowl and set aside to cool. Using the same hot frying pan, toss the grapes over the heat until blistered. Finish by drizzling over the pomegranate molasses to glaze them.

In a large bowl, place both the blistered grapes and sautéed garlic and spices. Add the chopped parsley, spring onions, tomatoes, cucumber, lemon zest/juice, dill, mint, sesame seeds and pistachios, and combine with the couscous. Gently mix through all the ingredients, seasoning with salt and pepper.

Take your salmon fillet and cut into 2.5cm cubes with skin on. Place into a large bowl with the olive oil and add all the other fish ingredients. Mix together.

Skewer the marinated salmon on soaked bamboo sticks, 4-5 pieces per skewer. Sprinkle with salt and barbeque for 2-3 minutes on each side.

Serve the salmon skewers with the couscous.

TIP: Remember to soak the bamboo skewers in water a couple of hours before barbequing so they don't burn.

SALMON FETTUCINE

I've given this traditional favourite a shake up! Who knew fettuccini could be light, summery, and hearty at the same time? Me!

FISH

400g **salmon fillet**, cubed and skin on

2 Tbsp **olive oil**

4 cloves **garlic**, chopped

8 **cherry tomatoes**, halved

8 **asparagus spears**, cut into 2.5cm pieces

1 Tbsp **capers**

¼ tsp **cracked pepper**

2 pinches of **flaky salt**

Juice of ½ **lemon**

250g **mascarpone cheese**

PASTA

500g **fresh fettucine**

2L **water**

Pinch of **salt**

1 tsp **olive oil**

2 Tbsp **olive oil**

TO SERVE

Parmesan, grated

Fresh herbs, chopped

Handful of **pine nuts**

Salmon roe (options)

In a large hot pan, use olive oil to lightly brown the garlic, cherry tomatoes and asparagus. Add the capers. Lower the heat and place the salmon cubes skin-side down into the pan to sear. Sprinkle cracked pepper and flaky salt over the salmon, cooking for 3-5 minutes until the skin is crispy. Squeeze the lemon juice over the fish, add the mascarpone cheese and stir in, turning over the salmon pieces. Simmer for 5-7 minutes. When the mascarpone turns a light golden colour it's ready to remove from the heat.

In a large saucepan, bring the water to the boil. Add the fresh fettucine with a pinch of salt and 1 teaspoon of olive oil. Boil for approx. 3 minutes.

Drain the pasta and return to the saucepan, stirring in 2 Tbsp olive oil.

Serve the creamy salmon sauce over the pasta with a sprinkle of parmesan, herbs, pine nuts and salmon roe.

TIP: If you can't get fresh fettucine, just use dried.

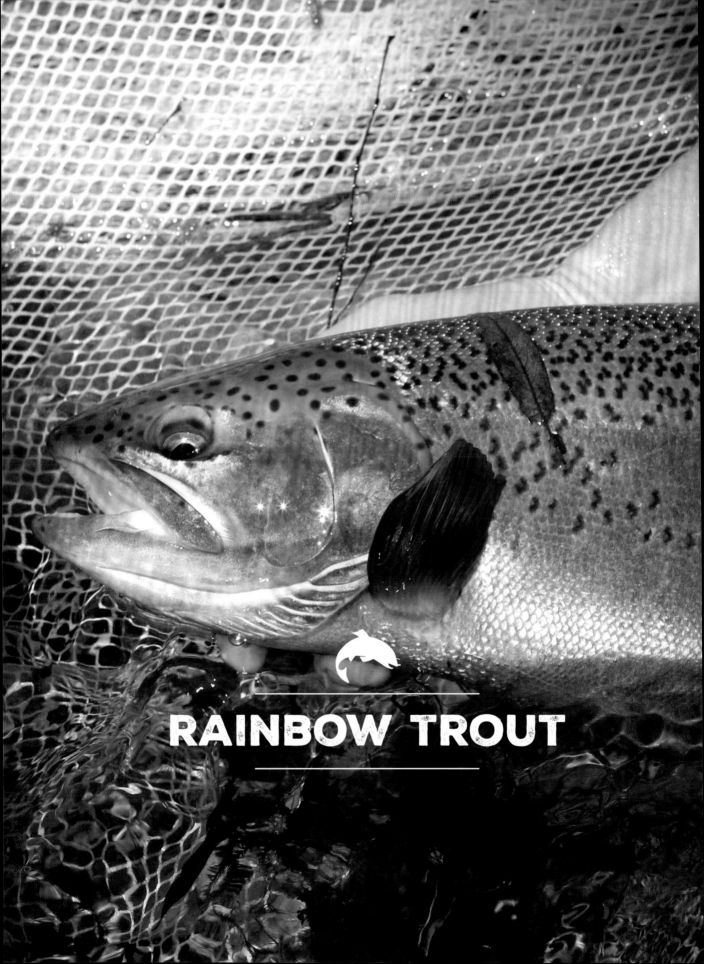

RAINBOW TROUT

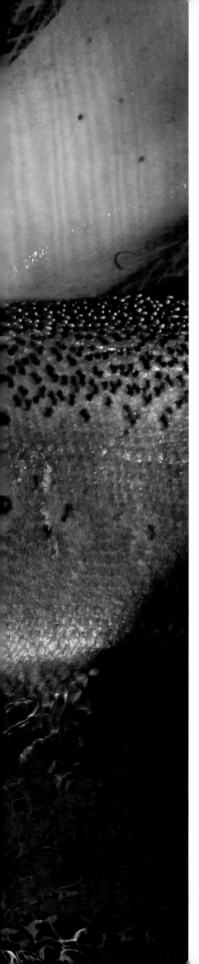

Rainbow trout took nearly two decades longer to establish in New Zealand than brown trout – but it was well worth the wait.

It wasn't until the 1880s that rainbow trout eggs were successfully imported from California after many disappointing failures.

Soon after the successful establishment of broodstock in Auckland, the Wellington Acclimatisation Society sent a letter in February of 1887 proposing to trade rainbow trout for perch or Loch Leven trout (brown trout).

Due to the fear that perch would likely destroy trout populations, it was decided that perch would not be released in the region.

That policy still stands today despite several illegal releases of perch occurring.

Brown trout are an excellent table fish, but the pink firm flesh of the rainbow trout make it a top choice for the table.

However, the vast majority of rainbow trout eaten around the world are commercially farmed rainbow trout.

The pink pigment in the flesh of wild rainbows is from carotenoids like astaxanthin, and it is the same pigment that gives flamingos their distinct colour.

Astaxanthin is produced by algae and eaten by small grazing invertebrates, working its way up the food chain to salmonids feeding on crustations like shrimp and freshwater crayfish.

Not all fish can convert carotenoids into their flesh, which is one reason why wild salmonids are so sought after.

To artificially produce pink flesh, farmed fish are fed carotenoids like astaxanthin that are predominantly produced synthetically.

Rainbow trout are easy to identify with a distinct pink stripe down the side of the fish starting at the gill plate that separates a green back covered in black spots from a silver belly.

Rainbows can be easily distinguished from Chinook salmon due to their white gums and from brown trout due to their pure black spots with no halos.

Spawning fish transition to a red body, but the gums will remain white.

Rainbow trout are one of the best fighting freshwater fish on the planet, second only to large salmon and steelhead.

Steelhead migrate offshore (whereas Chinook salmon follow the coastline), and the native ocean habitat of steelhead stays far cooler than the New Zealand coastline.

Unfortunately, the sea-running of steelhead was not a successful life-history trait in New Zealand despite the original California stock almost certainly coming from steelhead bloodstock.

It is likely that poor ocean conditions and possibly migration difficulties hampered the establishment of steelhead in New Zealand waters.

Adult rainbows typically weigh between 1-2kg in smaller streams, but in larger rivers and lakes, where food is abundant, they may reach 5kg or more.

But if rainbow trout can feed regularly, they can get enormous.

Trout and salmon in the canal fisheries of the central South Island feed on excess pellets from salmon farms and can grow to more than 19kg, making them amongst the biggest rainbow trout in the world.

– Dr Adam Daniel, Fish & Game New Zealand

RAINBOW IN A JAR

This is a brilliant and nutritious 'on the go' meal or snack! Easy to store for a rainy day or pack in your bag for those last minute fishing missions. Way better than canned fish!

FISH

1 **trout** (2 **fillets**), skin on

1 **bay leaf**, halved

2 cloves **garlic**, peeled

BRINE

¼ cup **apple cider vinegar**

¼ cup **water**

1 tsp **soft brown sugar**

1 tsp **kosher salt**

4 fronds **fresh dill**

10 **gourmet peppercorns**

¼ tsp **whole mustard seeds**

Sterilise 2 pickling jars and lids by boiling for 15 minutes. Then dry them in a hot oven for 10 minutes.

Tightly roll your fish fillets from tail to head with the skin showing. Drop or push each fillet into a jar (depending on the jar size). The idea is to remove as much air in the jars as possible by tightly packing the jars with the fillets. Place half a bay leaf and 1 whole clove of garlic into each jar.

To make the brine, in a saucepan add all the brine ingredients, bring to the boil and return to a simmer. Stir and simmer for 2 minutes. Remove from the heat, allow to cool for a few minutes and then pour the brine solution evenly between the jars. Tightly screw the lids on the jars.

In a pot, submerge the jars, covering them with 5cm of cold water. Bring to the boil, and boil for a minimum of 3 hours.

Turn off heat and allow the water to cool to a manageable temperature then carefully remove the jars from the saucepan and let rest on a tea towel to cool completely.

Store in a cool dry place.

Tastes great on a cracker!

TIP: If you're reusing any bottling/pickling jars and lids just make sure they're in good condition before use. Nobody wants trout brine juice leaking everywhere!

ANCHOVY BUTTERED RAINBOW TROUT WITH NEW POTATOES

Bring out the flavour of your freshly caught trout with this super easy, super fast, super tasty dish! Filling but light, it's a winner for the whole family.

POTATOES

14 **new potatoes**, halved

3 pinches of **salt**

FISH

2 **trout fillets**

75g **butter**

5 **anchovies**

2 cloves **garlic**, sliced

1 tsp **capers**

2 Tbsp **parsley**, chopped

1 Tbsp **dill**, chopped

Juice of ½ **lemon**

2 Tbsp **white wine**

3 Tbsp **cream**

2 pinches of **gourmet cracked peppercorns**

TO SERVE

Cracked peppercorns

Fresh parsley

In a saucepan, bring enough water to the boil to cover the potatoes, and boil until they are cooked through.

While the potatoes are cooking, in a hot frying pan, pan-sear the 2 trout fillets skin-side down in butter for about 3-5 minutes, adding the anchovies, garlic, capers, parsley and dill. Once the skin is crispy, squeeze lemon juice over the fish, flip it over and cook the other side for about 1 minute with the white wine. Remove the fish from the frying pan and set aside.

Once the potatoes are cooked, drain and add them to the hot frying pan. Pan-sear, tossing them through the herb infused anchovy butter. Add the cream and simmer for about 5 minutes or until the sauce thickens.

Serve with cracked peppercorns and parsley over the fish and creamy potatoes.

TIP: Place the trout skin-side down in the hot pan to create a lovely crispy skin.

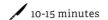
HERB-CRUSTED RAINBOW TROUT WITH BASIL & TOMATO SALAD

A little slice of Italy, this is a fresh favourite! If you can, use fresh herbs as that really brings out the delicate flavour of the fish and gives it that rustic Italian feel. Bellissima!

FISH

½ Tbsp **salted capers**

½ tsp **oregano**, chopped

½ tsp **parsley**, chopped

½ tsp **rosemary**, chopped

2 pinches of **lemon pepper**

1 Tbsp **panko bread crumbs**

1 **trout fillet**, skin on

3 Tbsp **olive oil**

DRESSING

1 Tbsp **white wine vinegar**

Juice of ½ **lemon**

2 Tbsp **extra virgin olive oil**

1 tsp **balsamic glaze**

2 **basil leaves**, finely chopped

SALAD

Handful of **asparagus spears**

200g **heirloom (or cherry) tomatoes**, quartered

¼ **red onion**, sliced

10 **basil leaves**

Salt & **pepper**

Preheat the oven on fan grill to 180°C.

In a bowl mix together the salted capers, fresh herbs, lemon pepper and panko crumbs.

Cut your fillet in half from head to tail, creating 2 narrower pieces. With the trout placed skin-side down, sprinkle the herbed crumb over the flesh and pat firmly with your fingers.

In a large hot oven-proof frying pan, add 2 Tbsp of olive oil and place the fish skin-side down. Drizzle an extra tablespoon of oil over the crumbed fillets. Pan-fry the fish for about 5 minutes until the skin is crispy (DO NOT turn the fillets over). Place the fillets in the oven to finish cooking under the grill for 10-12 minutes.

In a small bowl, add white wine vinegar, lemon juice, extra virgin olive oil, balsamic glaze and chopped basil. Mix thoroughly.

Take a handful of asparagus spears, chop into bite size pieces and drop into boiling water for 1 minute. Drain then cool.

In a bowl add the asparagus, tomatoes, red onion, basil leaves, salt and pepper. Toss through the dressing, coating the vegetables.

Serve with the crumbed trout.

TIP: If you don't have panko bread crumbs you can grate some slightly stale bread from the pantry instead.

BROWN TROUT

The golden prize of New Zealand's freshwater fish species, the brown trout is the most desired of our fish species and the hardest to catch.

The brown trout is a salmonid species of fish native to Europe, parts of North Africa and the Middle East that has long been viewed as a valuable sporting and table fish in its native range.

New Zealand's rivers and lakes, whilst possessing numerous native fish, have no native salmonids or comparable species.

And yet today, scarcely a waterway exists in New Zealand that is not, or at least was not at one stage, home to brown trout.

Over the course of the 150 years since their introduction in 1867, they have played a significant role in shaping not only New Zealand's environment but also aspects of its sporting culture.

Brown trout have become a valuable source of recreation and food for local anglers and the centrepiece of a significant international tourism industry.

Tens of thousands of anglers flock to New Zealand's waterways each year to pit their skills against these wily fish.

Furthermore, for early colonists, they represented both a strong connection to 'home' and also to the very lifestyle that many settlers left Britain for, and hoped to enjoy in New Zealand.

Travel by sea was the only option between New Zealand and Britain in the nineteenth century, and, in order to deliver trout ova, a ship would have to travel over 22,000km, across both tropics, in an age before refrigerated transportation.

Coupled with the sheer distance, trout are notoriously susceptible to changes in water temperature, as would occur when travelling with unrefrigerated shipping through tropical zones.

Finally, upon their arrival, there was no guarantee that the rivers and lakes of New Zealand would provide suitable habitats for brown trout.

A lack of understanding of the habitat requirements of trout also hampered introductions, especially in the North Island, where the Auckland Acclimatisation Society struggled to get trout to survive in the unsuitably warm climate – in Northland's Lake Omapere for example.

But find a home they did; now brown trout thrive wherever cool water habitats exist across the country.

They vary considerably in body colouration and markings depending on their habitat, making every brown trout you come across unique.

Sea-run brown trout, which enter the river mouths in pursuit of whitebait and smelt, are silver with a few dark, often indistinct marks which appear as small spots or crosses.

To the casual observer, large 'sea runs' can be incorrectly identified as sea-run salmon because of their silver appearance.

River resident brown trout are generally darker with brown or black spots, often surrounded by a pale halo.

Lake-dwelling brown trout frequently appear more silver than river fish.

Brown trout can be caught by various methods such as natural baits, spinners and wobblers, and artificial flies, including nymph, wet fly, feathered lure and dry fly.

They are warier than the rainbow trout, and, in a fly caster's opinion, it is the most difficult of the species to deceive with an artificial fly.

Despite this observation, there are more brown trout caught by anglers than any other species.

Large brown trout may attain a 10kg or more weight, although a fish over 5kg is considered a trophy.

– Dr Jack Kós, Fish & Game New Zealand

SHAKSHUKA WITH SMOKED BROWN TROUT

Spice up your breakfast with this lovely dish. If you have leftover trout, this is the perfect next morning meal! Plus the spices and red vegetables give you an antioxidant boost to kickstart your day.

FISH

150g **smoked trout fillets** (1 fish)

3 Tbsp **olive oil**

1 **sweet pepper**, sliced

8 **cherry tomatoes**, halved

¼ **red onion**, sliced

2 cloves **garlic**, sliced

½ cup **tomato passata sauce**

5 **eggs**

¼ tsp **ground cumin**

¼ tsp **ground smoked paprika**

¼ tsp **ground turmeric**

¼ tsp **ground coriander**

¼ tsp **cracked black pepper**

¼ tsp **salt**

1 Tbsp **fresh parsley**, chopped

½ Tbsp **fresh coriander leaves**, chopped

TO SERVE

Pita bread

Preheat the oven to 160°C.

Use a fork or your fingers to separate the trout flesh from the skin. Remove bones as you go. Set aside your fillet flakes in a bowl.

In a hot skillet, use 2 Tbsp olive oil to sauté the sweet pepper, cherry tomatoes, red onion and garlic for about 3 minutes or until golden brown. Transfer into a bowl and set aside.

Add 1 Tbsp oil to the same hot skillet. Lower the heat. Add the tomato passata sauce to the pan and crack the eggs on top. In a bowl combine all the spices and salt together, and sprinkle over the eggs and sauce.

Now gently return the sauteed vegetables to the skillet, being careful not to cover the egg yolks. Sprinkle the fresh parsley and coriander over the dish and add the trout fillet flakes on top, all the while keeping the egg yolks exposed.

Place in the oven and bake until the eggs are cooked to your liking.

Serve with warmed pita bread.

30 minutes   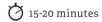 15-20 minutes   Serves 4

WHOLE SMOKED BROWN TROUT

Classic 'I caught my first fish' moment. Nothing beats a freshly smoked brown trout. The pinkish flesh melts in your mouth and will make a convert out of any first timer!

FISH

1 **large whole trout**, head removed, gutted, skin on and descaled

4-6 pinches of **flaky salt**

50ml **pomegranate molasses**

6 pinches of **smoked paprika**

4 pinches of **yellow mustard seeds**

10 fronds **dill**, chopped

10 **parsley leaves**, chopped

10 sprigs **thyme**, chopped

6 **mint leaves**, chopped

Zest of 1 **lemon**

1 clove **garlic**, sliced

1 **red chilli**, deseeded and sliced or alternatively use ¼ **red capsicum** (optional)

TO SERVE

Salad or **greens**

Set up your smoker.

Start by butterflying the whole trout. Once butterflied, pat the flesh dry with a paper towel. Place the butterflied trout skin-side down onto baking paper.

Sprinkle flaky salt and drizzle pomegranate molasses over the flesh. Continue by sprinkling smoked paprika, mustard seeds, chopped fresh herbs, lemon zest, garlic and chilli evenly over the fish.

Place in the smoker for about 15 minutes, checking every so often to see if it's cooked through.

Serve with salad or greens.

TIP: To butterfly the trout, run the knife down one side of the backbone, this way the backbone can be removed easily once cooked.

The Fish & Game Cookbook | Angelo Georgalli | BROWN TROUT

STICKY DATE BROWNIE

No, there's no chocolate in this recipe! But the dates give it a gorgeously rich sweetness in an otherwise savoury dish. It's a must-try – trust me, you'll be pleasantly surprised.

6 **medjool dates**, pitted

1 cup **orange juice**

1 **whole brown trout**, gutted, skin on and descaled

2 Tbsp **date syrup**

6 **mint leaves**

4 pinches of **flaky salt**

4 pinches of **pepper**

1 **mandarin**, sliced

Olive oil

Grab a handful of medjool dates, place in a small bowl with the orange juice and soak in the fridge overnight.

Preheat the oven to 170°C.

Keeping the whole fish intact, place on baking paper and score along one side of the fish using a sharp knife. Repeat on the other side.

Brush the whole fish with the date syrup, making sure the syrup soaks into the flesh of the fish through the scored incisions and brush inside the gut cavity.

Taking your orange soaked dates, quarter them and place the quarters with the mint leaves into the scored incisions along the body of the fish. Season with salt and pepper. Repeat on the other side. Now take the mandarin slices and stuff into the gut cavity,

Drizzle olive oil over the fish and place in the oven for 20-25 minutes or until cooked.

Serve as is, being mindful of bones.

TIP: Scoring the fish simply means to slice incisions along the body of the fish from the dorsal fin down to the belly, creating the look of gills along the whole body of the fish. A great technique for infusing flavour.

PERCH

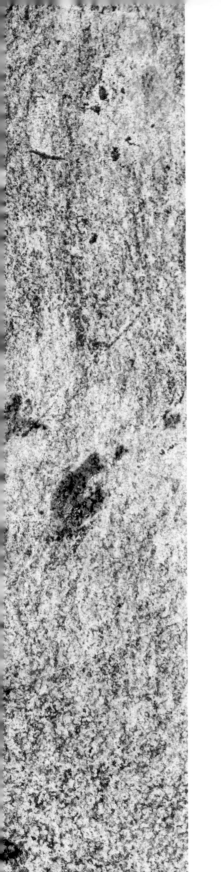

The perch is an excellent eating fish, and its white flesh is considered a delicacy by restaurant chefs worldwide.

Many anglers often describe the taste as the freshwater equivalent of blue cod.

The first perch arrived in New Zealand in 1868 in Otago; they were released widely throughout New Zealand and quickly became established.

But interest in them declined rapidly once brown trout became successfully established, even though they are arguably the better-eating fish.

Perch are usually very numerous wherever they are found, and consequently, the fish are, on average, ideally sized for the plate.

However, large perch have been caught, in some cases weighing up to 2.2kg.

Many Kiwis use perch as an easily accessible food source for their families.

Perch is a deep-bodied fish with two large and erect dorsal fins, the first fin having an array of strong and sharp spines.

There are two other less obvious spines on each gill cover, which quickly become known to the unwary angler who handles their catch carelessly!

The pelvic and anal fins and the lower half of the tail are orange-red. The olive-green back is tiger-striped by six or seven dark bands which extend down to a silver/white belly.

Perch like still water and often frequent the shallows, especially where there are underwater structures or snags such as tree roots or jetty piers.

Smaller perch swim in small schools; larger fish are usually solitary.

Perch are easy to catch; they are particularly attracted to the colour red, though they are not caught during the hours of darkness, and they will take natural baits and spin baits with great vigour.

They are an aggressive feeding fish and an excellent introductory fish for novice anglers to harvest, being plentiful and easy to find.

It is important to stress that perch love structures in the water; if there are jetties and piers in the vicinity, then target these areas.

As ambush predators, they love hiding out near or around them, ready to pounce on any unsuspecting prey.

Because of this, anglers will also find targeting the lake edges a very productive technique, either from shore or boat.

Unlike many fish species, perch are not put off by boat activity; in fact, as this activity often stirs up smaller fish, they are often attracted to boat movements in the hope of catching smaller unsuspecting fish species.

They also become more active as the water temperature warms up, making perch fishing an ideal summer holiday activity for young anglers.

Whereas in hot temperatures, trout and salmon will be seeking cooler, deeper waters, perch, in contrast, will be much more active in warmer water.

Remember to move around to find the fish; around the corner, there might just be a school of perch waiting.

As they're so aggressive, most fishing methods will work to catch them. Spinning lures, soft baits, and bubble floats – all will catch perch.

– Richard Cosgrove, Fish & Game New Zealand

PERCH CEVICHE

This delightful summer dish is well suited to the texture of perch, giving you a light, fresh, and totally scrumptious balance of flavours.

FISH

200g **perch fillets**, chopped into 1cm cubes

Juice of 1 **lime**

¼ **red chilli**, finely sliced

½ cup **coconut milk**

4 pinches of **salt**

2 pinches of **cracked pepper**

¼ **cucumber**, shaved

10 **cherry tomatoes**, halved

¼ **red capsicum**, finely sliced

½ handful of **fresh coriander leaves**, roughly chopped

2 **spring onions**, finely sliced

¼ **red onion**, finely sliced

2 fronds **dill**

TO SERVE

1 Tbsp **pomegranate seeds**

1 Tbsp **black sesame seeds**

½ Tbsp **extra virgin olive oil**

Put the cubed perch fillets into a bowl and squeeze over the lime juice. Add the chilli slices and refrigerate for 30 minutes. The fillets should look opaque and white once ready. Pour the coconut milk into the bowl, adding salt and pepper.

In a separate bowl toss the shaved cucumber, cherry tomatoes, red capsicum, coriander, spring onions, red onion and dill together.

Combine the coconut fish mixture with the sliced salad and gently toss through with your hands.

Serve into a bowl and garnish with pomegranate and black sesame seeds and dress with extra virgin olive oil.

TIP: Be very careful when handling the fish as the dorsal fin and gill plate are very spikey. I suggest using a tea towel to handle the fish.

GREEK PAN-FRIED PERCH WITH SPINACH HUMMUS

The traditional diet of many Mediterranean countries is heavy in fish, tomatoes, olive oil, and hummus. My father, a Cypriot Greek, would have absolutely loved this recipe. Papa, this one's for you!

FISH

1 **perch fillet**, skin off

2 Tbsp **extra virgin olive oil**

1 clove **garlic**, sliced

¼ **red onion**, sliced

¼ **zucchini**, sliced

8 **kalamata olives**

1 pinch of **lemon pepper**

1 pinch of **fennel seeds**

Salt & **pepper**

Juice of ½ **lemon**

TO SERVE

½ handful of **fresh mint leaves**

Spinach Hummus (see page 36)

In a large hot frying pan, brown the garlic, red onion, zucchini and kalamata olives in extra virgin olive oil. Add the lemon pepper and fennel seeds, and season with salt and pepper.

Next, season the fish with salt and pepper, and fry in the pan for about 5 minutes or until cooked through. Squeeze lemon juice over the fish and remove from the heat.

Garnish with mint leaves and serve on a bed of spinach hummus.

TIP: I tend to use extra virgin olive oil in this recipe because it gives it a full rich flavour, which works really well with this style of dish.

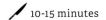
PERCH & POTATO CURRY

Everyone loves a hearty fish curry and this one won't disappoint. Perch fillets are perfect for curry, creating a gorgeous blend of texture, fragrance, and taste.

FISH

300g **perch fillets**, skin off

2 Tbsp **vegetable oil**

500g **potatoes**, chopped

1 **red onion**, sliced

¼ tsp **cumin**

¼ tsp **turmeric**

¼ tsp **ground coriander seeds**

1 **zucchini**, sliced

1 litre **Fish Stock** (see page 34)

2 Tbsp **tomato paste**

Salt

½ **lime**

Fish Rub (see page 35)

TO SERVE

Fresh coriander leaves, roughly chopped

Rice, cooked

Into a large bowl smother the perch fillets in fish rub, ensuring the fillets are completely covered. Marinate overnight in the fridge.

To make the curry: in a large hot saucepan sauté the potatoes, onion and spices in the vegetable oil until golden brown. Add the zucchini and fry-off for a little longer, then add the fish stock. Turn the heat down to a simmer. Stir in the tomato paste. Add salt to taste and cook for about 30 minutes.

Place your marinated fish fillets into the curry with half a lime and its juice. Simmer for a further 10 minutes, being careful not to over-cook as the fillets will lose their structure.

Serve with fresh coriander leaves and a bowl of rice.

Any leftovers will refrigerate in an airtight container for 3-4 days.

TIP: The potatoes should be cooked through and soft in the centre before adding the fish.

FENNEL & GRAPE PAN-FRIED PERCH WITH PICKLED CUCUMBER & YOGHURT

Fresh, zesty, simple, and yummy! An easy-to-prepare combination for a perfect summery meal! The yoghurt dip gives the perch a real zing!

PICKLE

Pickled Cucumber (see page 35)

YOGHURT DIP

3 Tbsp **Greek yoghurt**

Squeeze of **lemon juice**

½ clove **garlic**, minced

2 pinches of **pepper**

Pinch of **salt**

Pinch of **ground cumin**

Pinch of **ground turmeric**

Pinch of **smoked paprika**

½ handful of **parsley**, chopped

FISH

2 **perch fillets**, skin removed

1 Tbsp **olive oil**, plus extra drizzle

8 **grapes**, halved

1 clove **garlic**, sliced

¼ **fennel** bulb, sliced

¼ **sweet red pepper**, sliced

2 pinches of **salt**

2 pinches of **cracked black pepper**

1 **lemon** wedge

TO SERVE

Extra virgin olive oil

Fresh dill fronds

Slice of **lemon**

In a bowl, combine the yoghurt dip ingredients and mix well. Refrigerate until ready to serve.

In a hot frying pan, lightly brown the grapes, garlic, fennel and sweet pepper in olive oil. Season with salt and pepper.

Add the fillets to the hot pan with a further drizzle of olive oil. Squeeze then add the lemon wedge to the pan. Pan-fry the fish on both sides until cooked through.

Remove from the heat and plate up with a helping of pickled cucumbers and a dollop of yoghurt dip.

Drizzle with extra virgin olive oil, and garnish with a slice of lemon and fresh dill.

TIP: It's best to make your pickled cucumber at least the night before to allow the cucumbers to completely pickle before eating them.

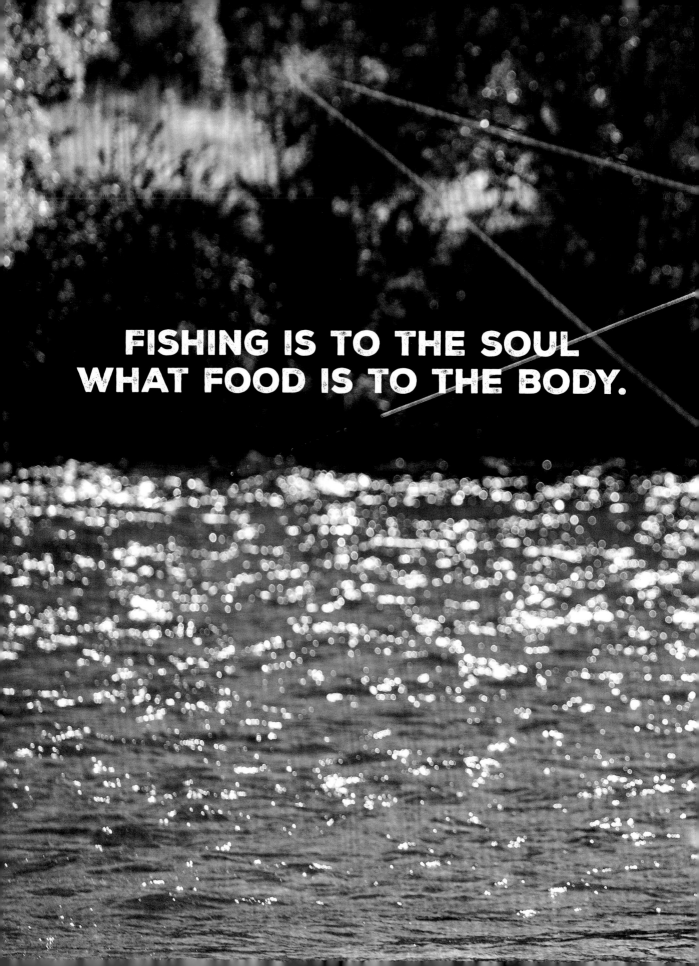

FISHING IS TO THE SOUL
WHAT FOOD IS TO THE BODY.

FOOD PHOTOGRAPHY SHOOT LOCATION: LAKE HĀWEA STATION

The mountains and valleys that make up the terrain of Lake Hāwea Station are an extreme kind of beautiful. Almost mystical. I can only imagine what early settlers to the region must have thought. Stunning, vivid, treacherous. I know this because I thought it myself when I first saw the eastern shores of Lake Hāwea, a renowned angling haven just 30 minutes' drive from Wānaka. It's a landscape that tweaks the heartstrings of any hunter, any outdoor enthusiast. A deep, clear lake fed from glaciers and mountain streams, where rainbow and brown trout flourish. Sharp angled peaks and sheer ravines are the perfect domain for the numerous wild goats, tahr, and red deer. And holding court at the head of the lake is Lake Hāwea Station. The homestead and its farmland take high country station to the next level.

Since new owners, Geoff, Justine, Finn and Gabe Ross, bought the farm in 2018, they have been carefully and conscientiously regenerating the land and have committed to a new and profoundly liberating way to farm. They get it, the delicate balance in nature, holding it as deeply as I hold my own strong values and wild kitchen philosophy, which is one of the reasons I was so thrilled to stay at one of their bespoke cottages, using it as a base for many of the recipe creations you'll see in this book. I have always loved the Lake Hāwea region, and I'm privileged to have met the Ross family and learned about how they are nurturing the land and opening it up to others to learn to do the same. Like me, they know the value of every part of a plant or creature, and they respect, and are honoured to be custodians of, such a unique and special place.

FISH & GAME SIGN-OFF

Fish & Game play a guardianship role in New Zealand for the species harvested and cooked by Angelo in the making of this cookbook. We hope you take the opportunity to harvest and enjoy the bounty available to you in our vast open spaces. This cookbook was inspired by Angelo and the long history of angling and game bird hunting managed by Fish & Game.

Wild food usually comes because of an adventure, and it is so perfectly rounded off by some time in the kitchen or around the campfire with an inspirational meal caught and cooked by you.

We encourage you to experiment with your wild-harvested food. Angelo has taken the fear out of cooking game birds and sports fish throughout these pages and shown that the flavours you'll experience with our game birds and sports fish are far better than most would ever believe possible. The beautiful dishes (to the tastebuds and the eye) that Angelo has created are an inspiration for us all to get out there and try something new.

This cookbook wouldn't exist without the ability to harvest these fantastic wild species in New Zealand. Anglers and hunters each year enable future generations to continue the wild kai traditions of our forebears and go out there hunting and fishing, with a licence of course.

Fish & Game is totally licence fee funded. We use those licence fees carefully to manage, maintain and enhance hunting and angling opportunities across the country.

It's a responsibility we take incredibly seriously. Often, it's incredibly detailed, hard, tedious work, doing things like: attending resource consent hearings to protect habitat, restoring habitat, negotiating access for anglers and hunters, and conducting enforcement operations to protect the resource from poaching.

This cookbook wouldn't be the success it is without the help of a bunch of people from the wider Fish & Game family.

They have given their time, knowledge and advice to help make this book come together.

A huge thanks to: Stu Henderson, Colin Hewson, Dean Rattray, Tracy Morrow, Ben Sowry, Hayden Glover, Hayden Roberts, Hamish Stevens, Rhys Adams, Dan & Elizabeth Isbister, Ken & Fiona Bowmar, John Dyer, Jayde Couper, John Meikle, Mark Sherburn, Adam Daniel, Baylee Kersten, Jack Kos, Jarrad Melhopt, Steve Doughty and Richard Cosgrove.

– Dianna Taylor, Fish & Game New Zealand

CHEERS FROM ANGELO

Well, what can I say. A third cookbook and so many people to thank for helping me make it happen. Honestly, this is my dream, being able to spend time creating recipes and experiment with flavours that enhance the natural taste of wild game in New Zealand – it's a privilege I don't take lightly.

First off, a massive thank you to the farmers who helped find the right locations for the photography of our action shots. Allowing us onto your land, to fish or shoot, well, we couldn't have made this book happen without your support, so thank you so much.

To High Country Salmon NZ – guys, your salmon is just amazing! Thank you so much for supplying two whole salmon so that I could get these recipes right! If I'd fished for all the salmon myself, this cookbook might have taken a bit longer to produce!

To Boh & Ivy Ltd in Wānaka, your plates and accessories look incredible in the imagery throughout this book and we are so grateful to have been able to use them. Thank you.

To the folks at the good old Mediterranean Market in Wānaka, you guys have been providing the best quality ingredients and supplies to me for years. Thank you for your commitment to keeping things as local as possible and for sourcing those marvellous ingredients from around the world.

To Epic Fly Fishing – thanks for the tackle, team! Good stuff! Your sponsorship of tackle helped me catch the fish you see right here in this book!

To Berretta NZ, thank you so much for the 687 Upland Game 12 gauge shotgun. This beauty was instrumental in being able to create many of my recipes here. If it missed the target, it certainly wasn't the fault of the gun! Cheers guys!

Hey, Kevin Duncan, thank you mate, for inspiring me to try out my bottled rainbow trout recipe. It worked a treat! Even made it into the book!

Phil Jarratt, for my hand-crafted kitchen knife, it's absolutely beautiful. A trusty companion in creating all the recipes you see here.

Lake Hāwea Station, what can I say. Your property, your ethos, the way you're changing the way high country farming is done, I take my hat off to you and thank you so very much for being able to use your stunning accommodation for our first location.

My deepest gratitude and thanks to the team at Beatnik Publishing for making this cookbook possible. Sally, you are a star and, with every cookbook we work on, I am just amazed at your talent in bringing it all together.

To the incredible Carla Munro, your writing, I don't know how you do it, but it's like you hear my voice in your head and the words just come out exactly as I want to say them. As the creative writer behind this and every one of my cookbooks, I thank you from the bottom of my heart for helping me express what I want to say.

To the amazing team at Fish & Game New Zealand, a huge thanks to Richard Cosgrove, Steve Doughty and everyone else involved, your collaboration in helping put this book together has been epic. What you do for this beautiful country and the people in it, it's just brilliant, guys, it really is. The shooting and fishing memories will stay with me always.

And finally, to Sky for all your support along the way in helping materialise this cookbook. As my Recipe Development Assistant you have outdone yourself. You're a keeper. X

RECIPE INDEX